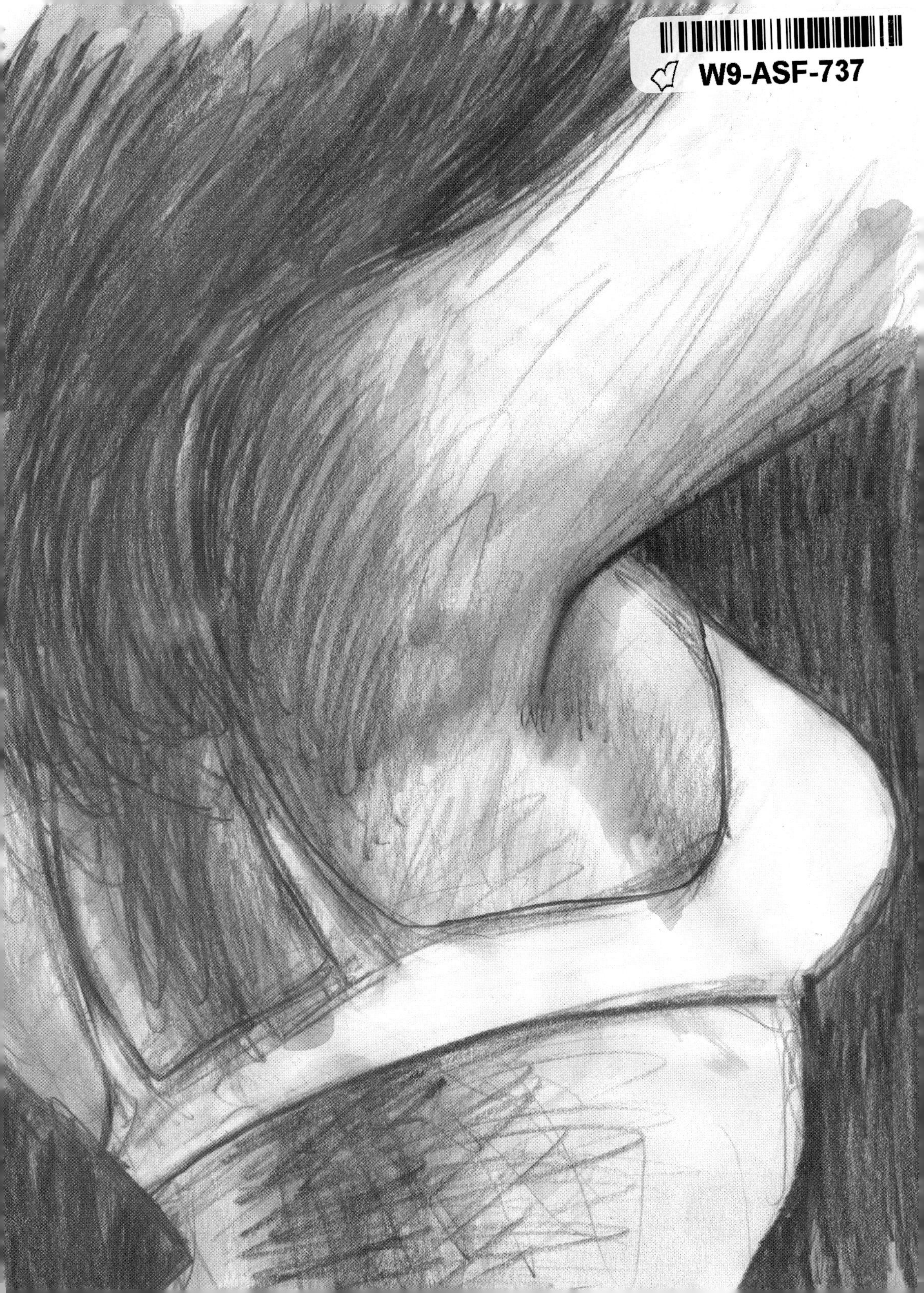

© Jimmy Beaulieu, 2014

First English Edition

Original French edition © Jimmy Beaulieu and mécanique générale / Les 400 Coups, 2006

Translation by KerryAnn Cochrane
BDANG Imprint edited by Andy Brown
Printed by Gauvin Press in Quebec, Canada

Library and Archives Canada Cataloguing in Publication

Beaulieu, Jimmy, 1974-
[Ma voisine en maillot. English]
    My neighbour's bikini / Jimmy Beaulieu.

(Bdang)
Translation of: "Ma voisine en maillot".
ISBN 978-1-894994-83-5 (pbk.)

    1. Graphic novels. I. Title. II. Title: Ma voisine en
maillot. English. III. Series: Bdang imprint series

PN6734.M3B4213 2014   741.5'971   C2014-900407-9

BDANG IMPRINT #14

CONUNDRUM PRESS

Greenwich, Nova Scotia, Canada
www.conundrumpress.com

Conundrum Press acknowledges the financial support of the Canada Council for the Arts toward its publishing activities. We acknowledge the financial support of the Government of Canada, through the National Translation Program for Book Publishing, for our translation activities.

Canada Council
for the Arts
Conseil des Arts
du Canada

my neighbour's bikini

Jimmy Beaulieu

"If I'm troubled by every folding of your skirt,
Am I guilty of every male inflicted hurt?"

— Paddy McAloon

My only regret when it comes to creating graphic novels, as opposed to movies or plays, is that it's impossible to knit sound into them. If I could, I would have started with "Wives & Lovers" by Bacharach / David, sung by Dionne Warwick. Then, for pages 5 to 13, it would be the theme song from "Fantomas" by Michel Magne. It would change, for pages 14 to 26, to a ride with some crackling brass, solidly accompanied by a musician's fingers walking up and down the strings of a double bass. Pages 27 to 37 would contain the full instrumental version of "Wives & Lovers" by Bacharach on his own. Pages 38 to 41 would be "The Man with the Golden Arm" by Barry Adamson. Pages 45 and 46 would be "Beat Surrender" by The Jam (softly, to start). And I'd finish with The Jesus & Mary Chain and their piece "Moe Tucker" (yes, that's the one). If you are resourceful, you'll be able to find excerpts from these pieces on the Internet.

— Jimmy Beaulieu

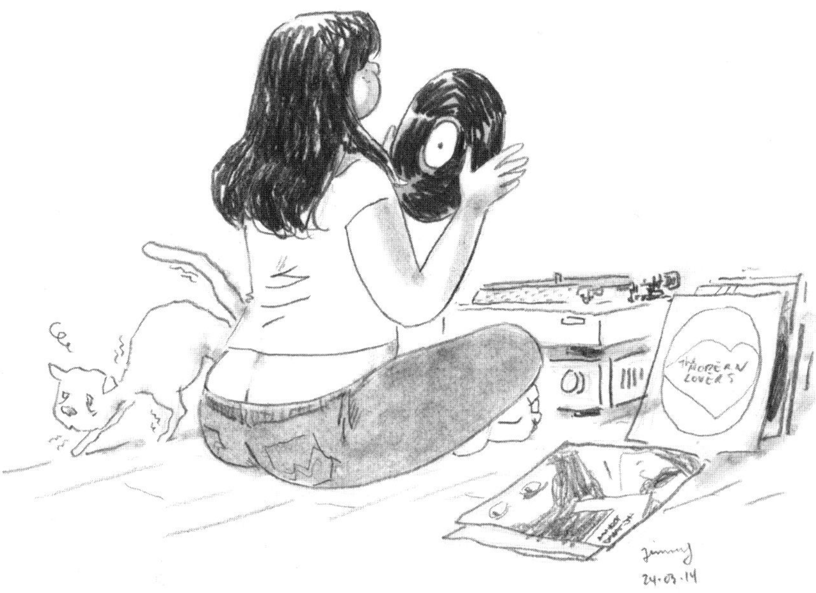
THE MODERN LOVERS
Jimmy
24.03.14

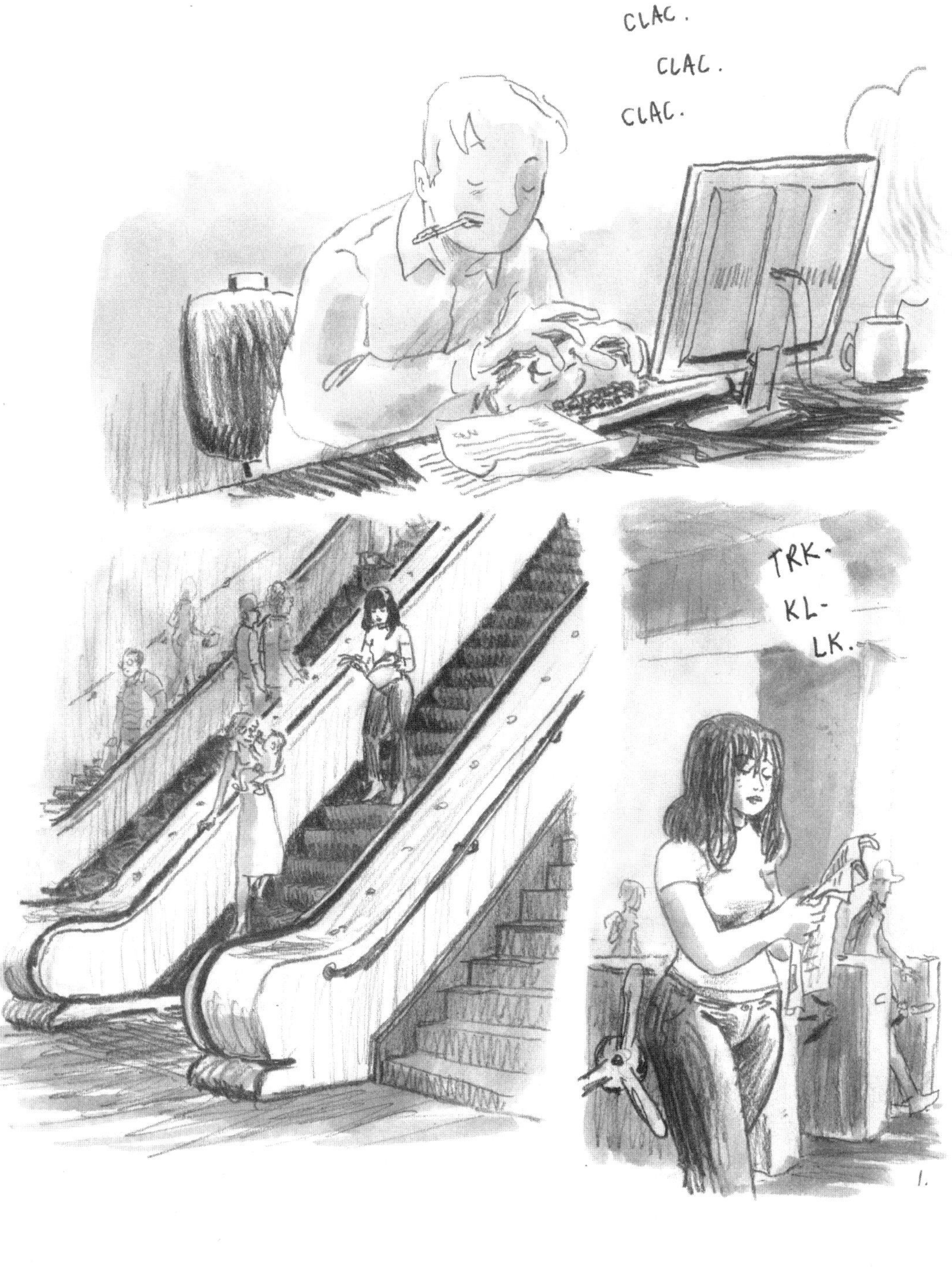
CLAC.
CLAC.
CLAC.
TRK-
KL-
LK.

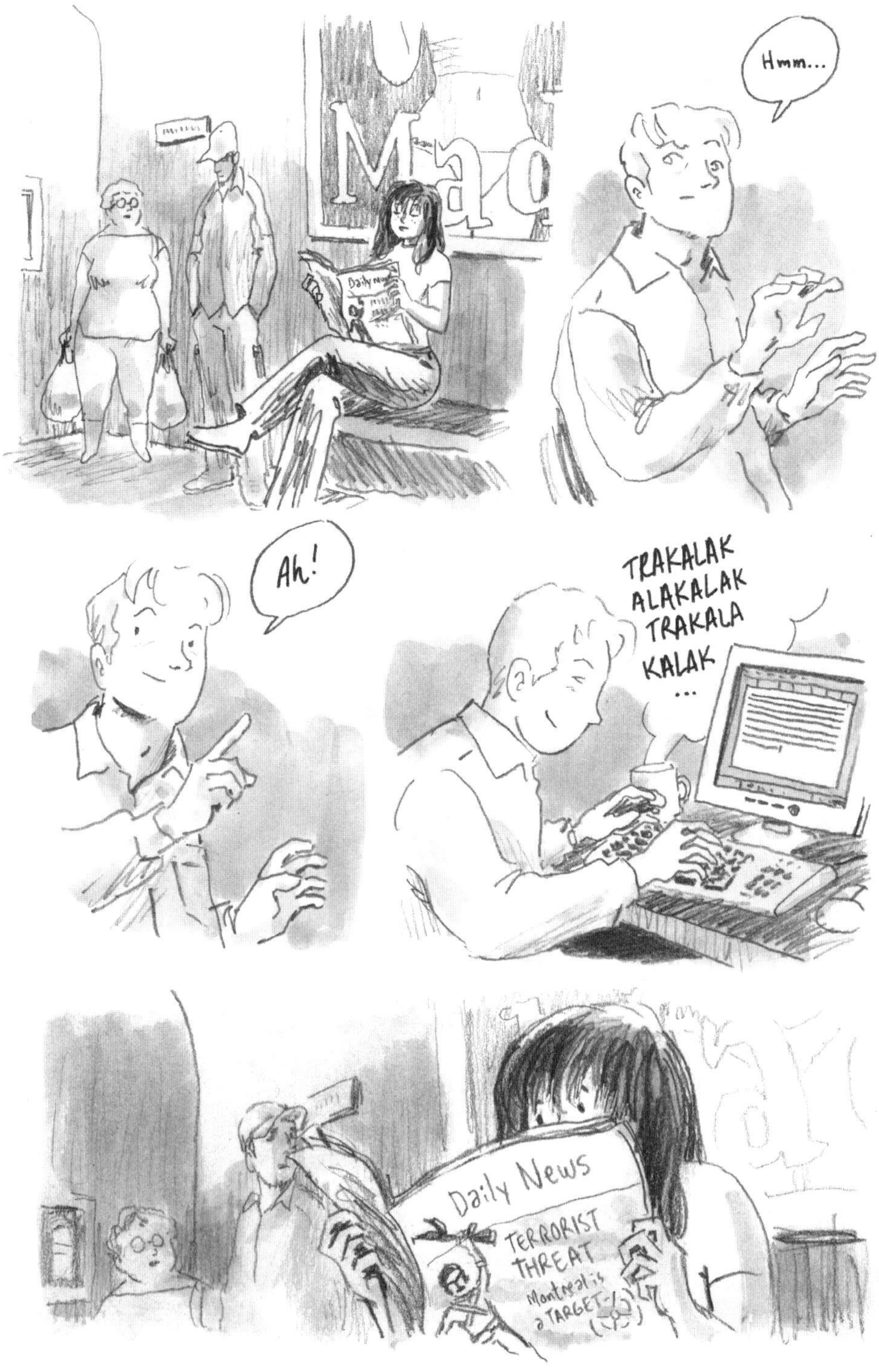
Hmm...
Ah!
TRAKALAK
ALAKALAK
TRAKALA
KALAK
...
Daily News
TERRORIST
THREAT
Montreal is
a TARGET-!

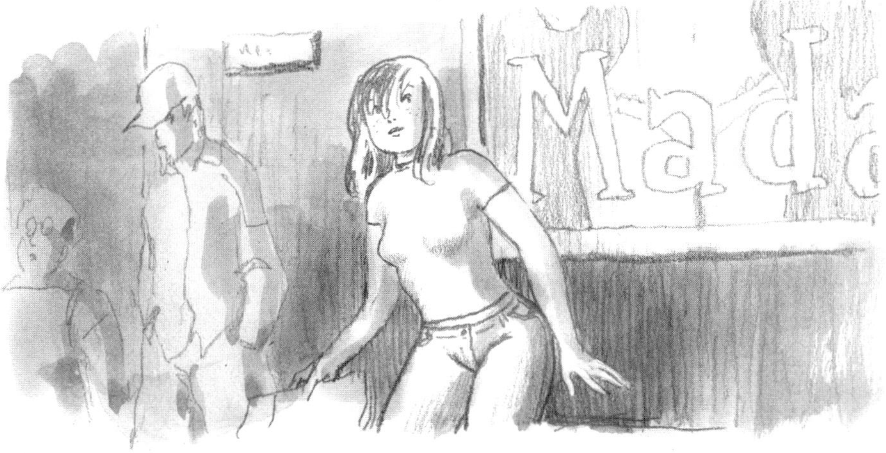

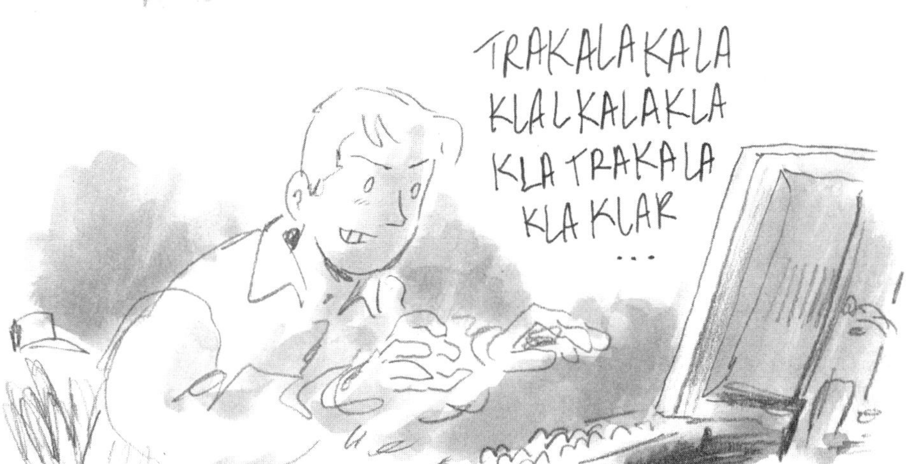
TRAKALAKALA
KLALKALAKLA
KLA TRAKALA
KLA KLAR
...

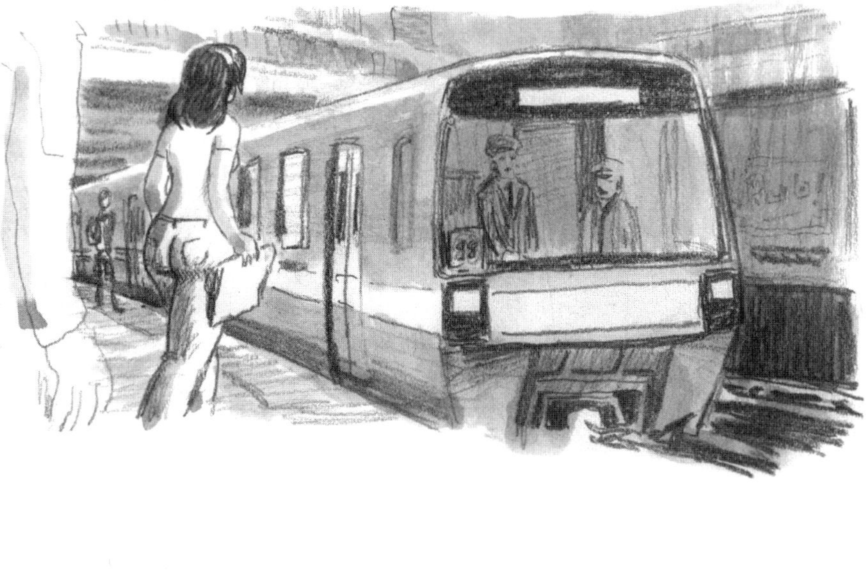

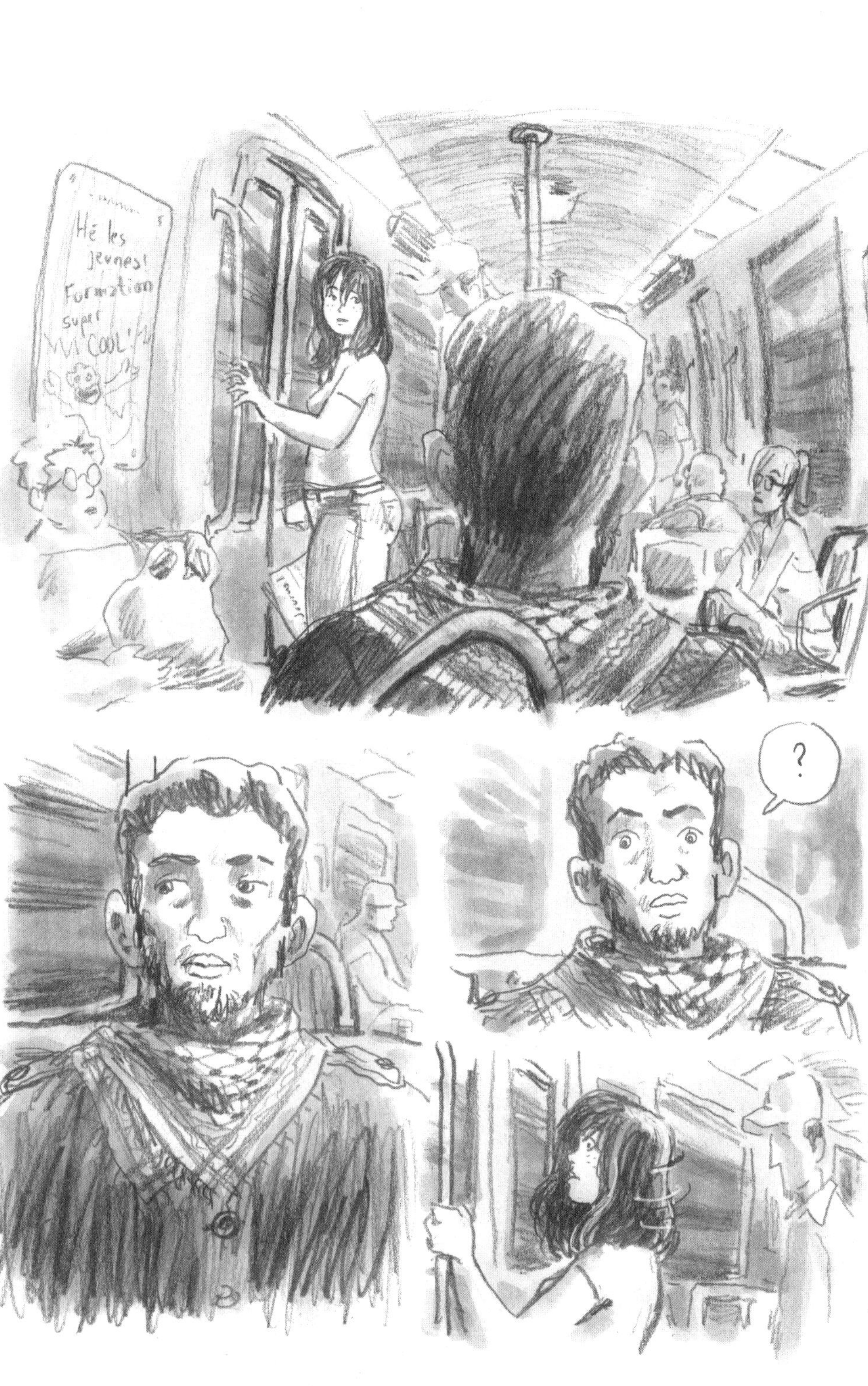
Hé les jeunes!
Formation super COOL!
?

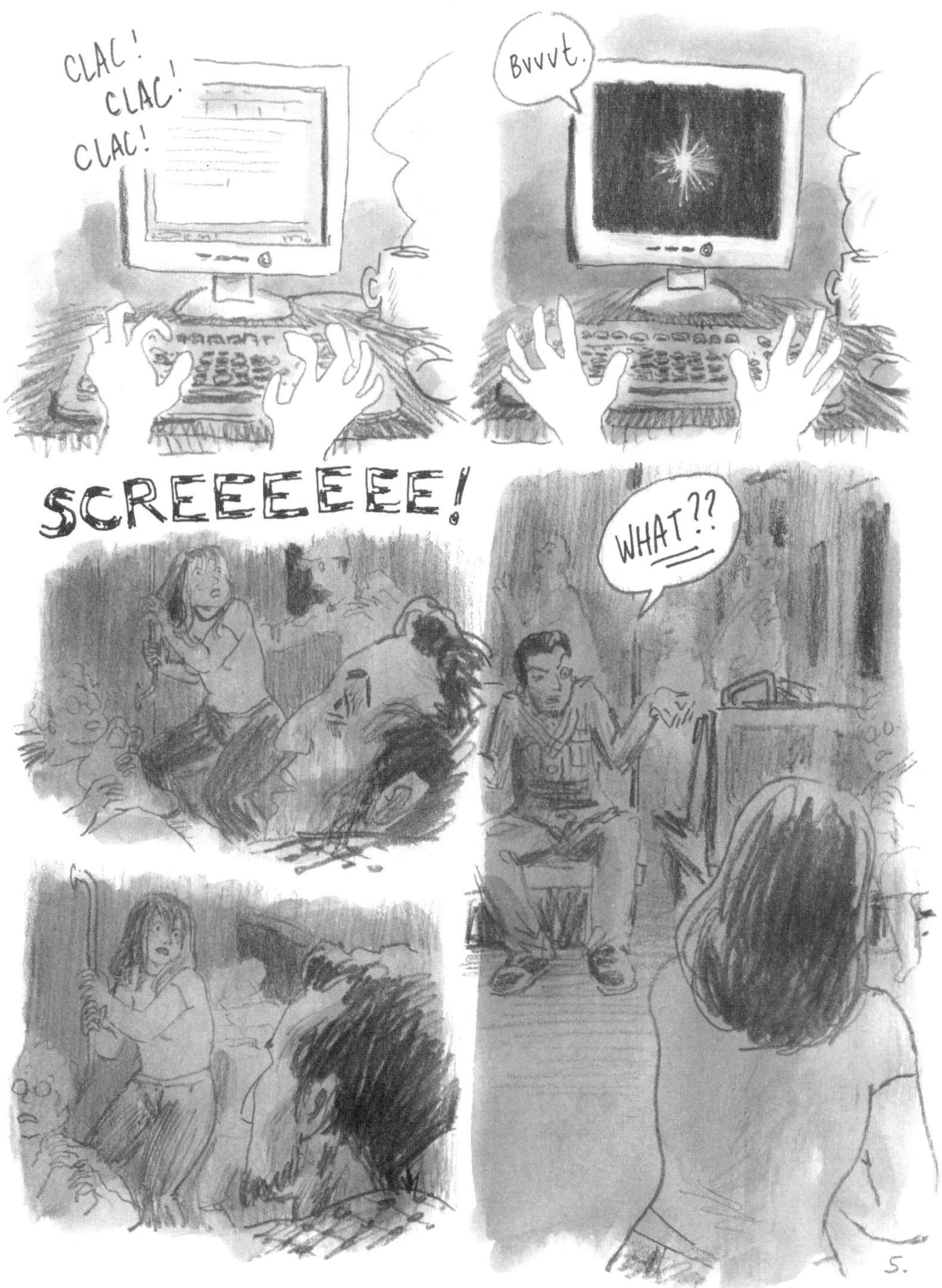
CLAC!
CLAC!
CLAC!
Bvvvt.
SCREEEEEEE!
WHAT??

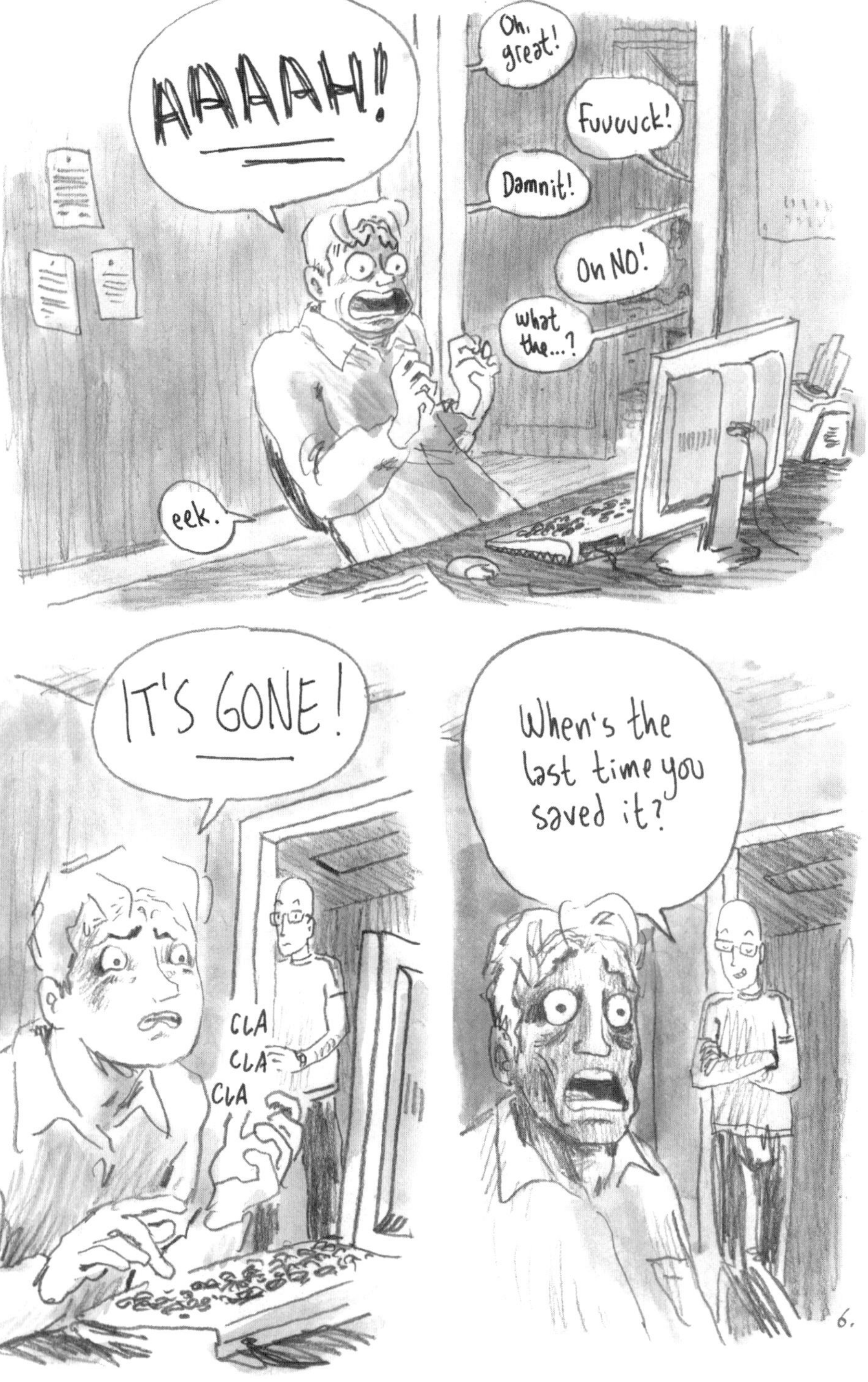
AAAAH!
Oh, great!
Fuuuuck!
Damnit!
Oh NO!
what the...?
eek.
IT'S GONE!
CLA
CLA
CLA
When's the last time you saved it?

Whadda ya think? I didn't even save it once all day!...
And you know that if I HAD, there wouldn't be a power outage ...
If it comes back soon, maybe I'll be able to remember the most important parts...
Ha Ha! Always the optimist!!!
Don't we have a generator? Bloody hell...
Um, nope. We don't.
Is it just our building or the whole neighbourhood?

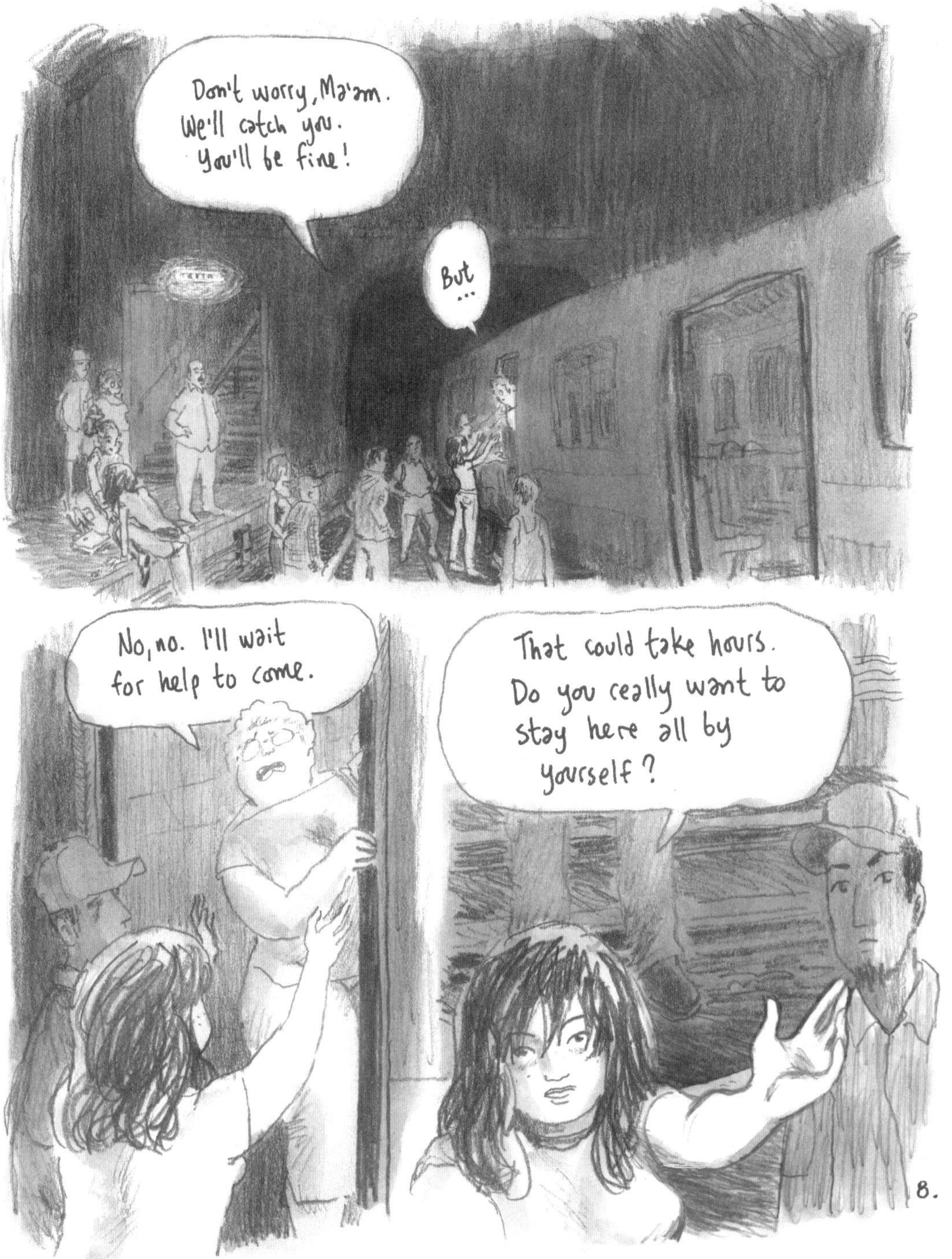
Don't worry, Ma'am. We'll catch you. You'll be fine!
But ...
No, no. I'll wait for help to come.
That could take hours. Do you really want to stay here all by yourself?

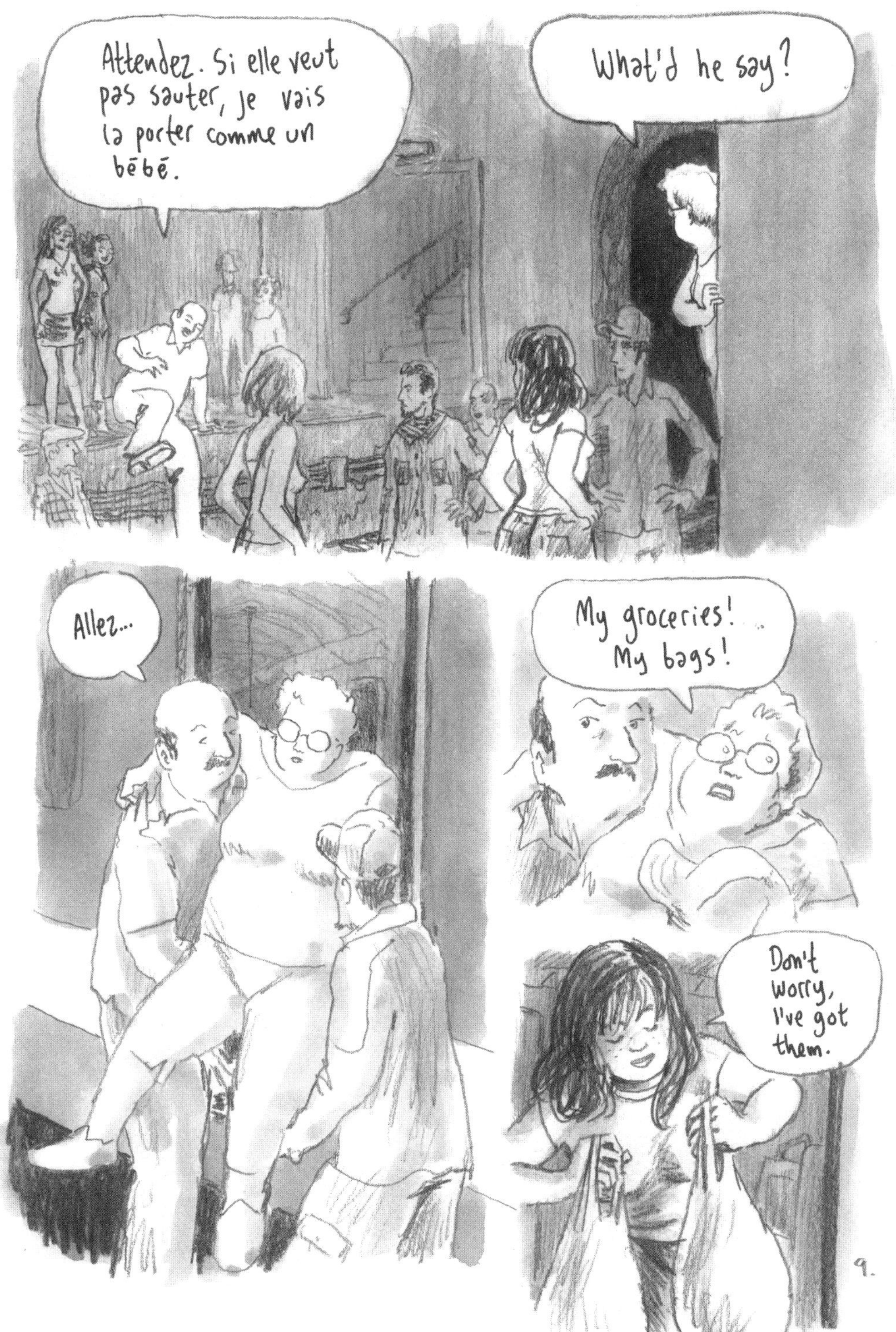
Attendez. Si elle veut pas sauter, je vais la porter comme un bébé.
What'd he say?
Allez...
My groceries! My bags!
Don't worry, I've got them.

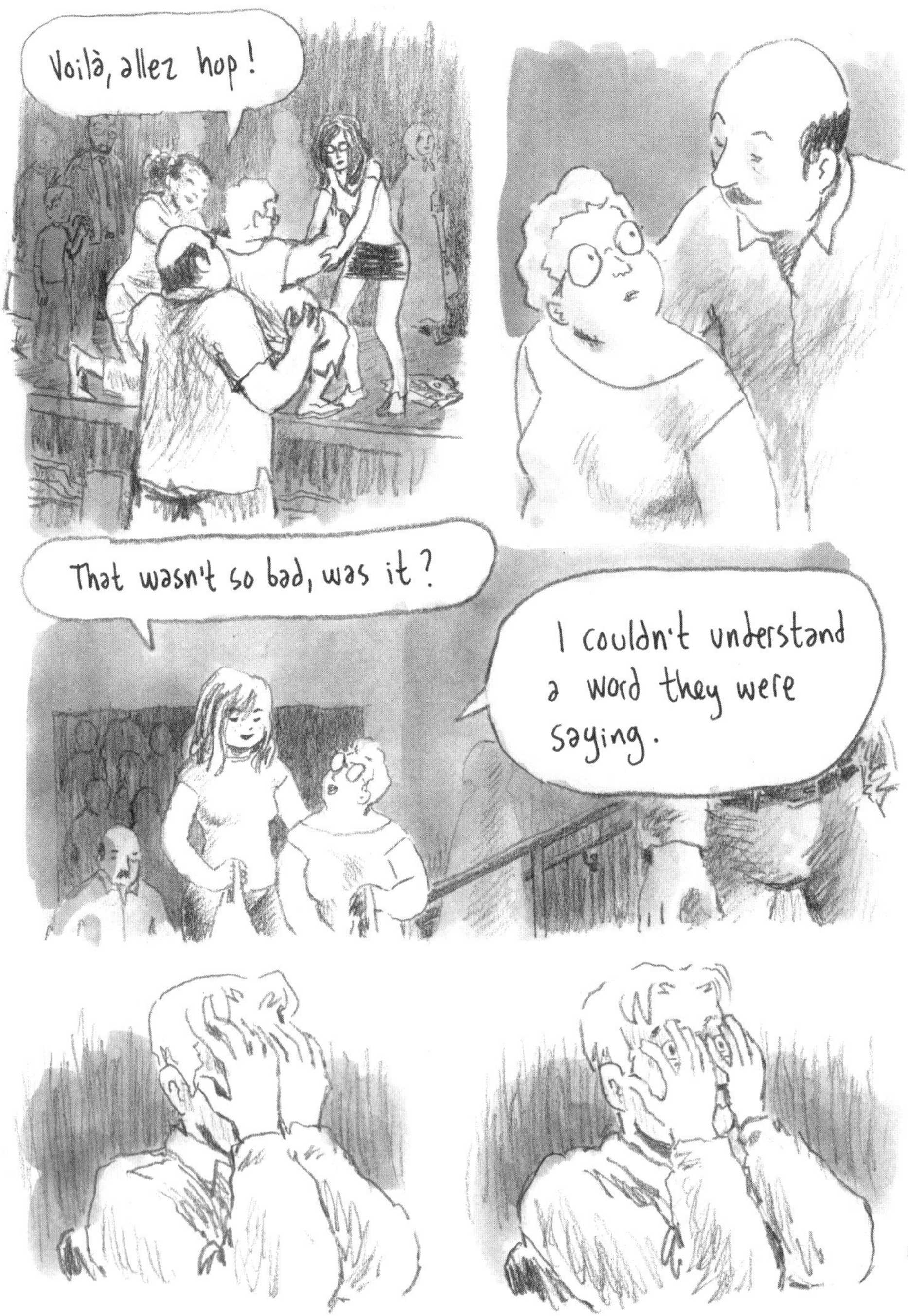
Voilà, allez hop!
That wasn't so bad, was it?
I couldn't understand a word they were saying.

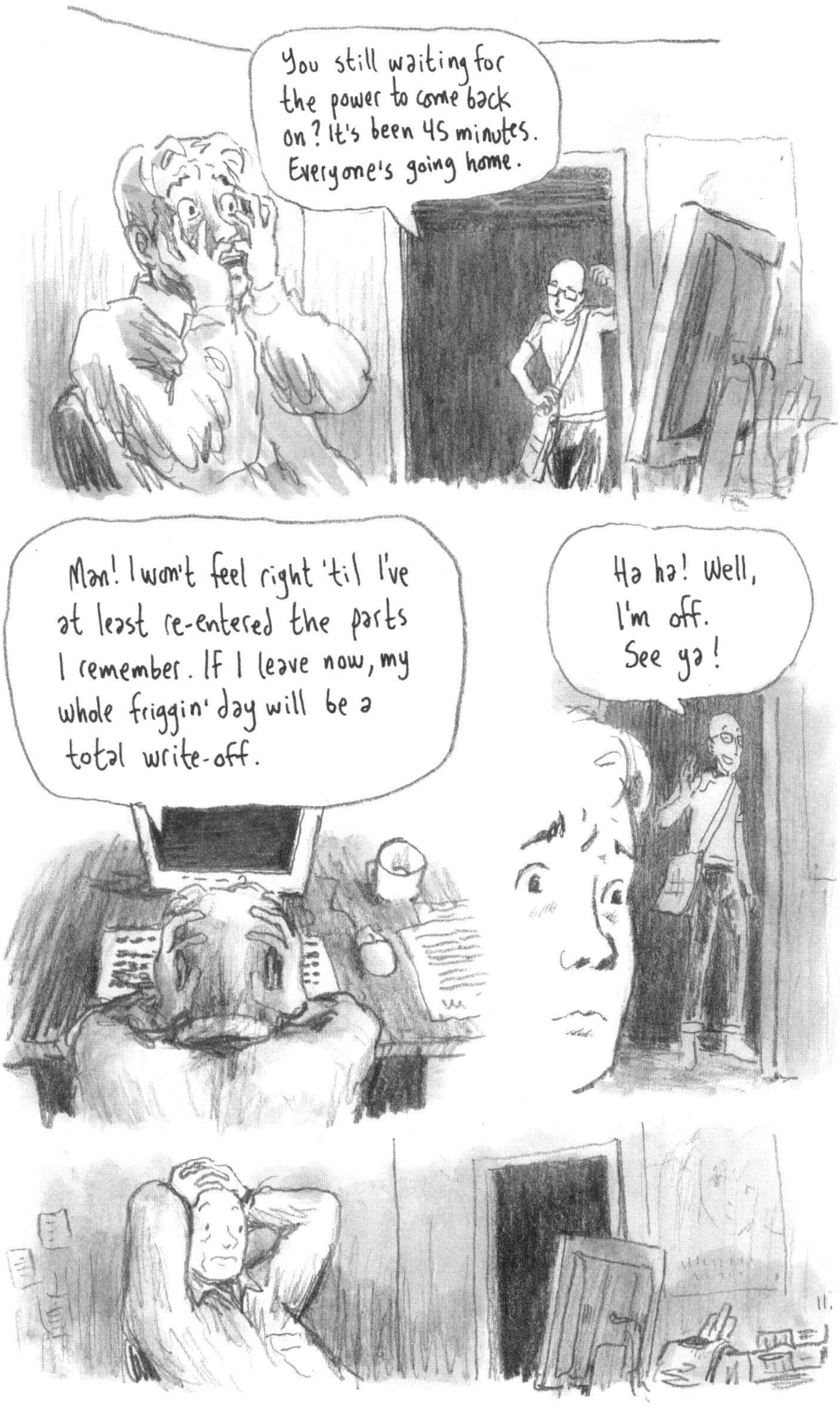
You still waiting for the power to come back on? It's been 45 minutes. Everyone's going home.
Man! I won't feel right 'til I've at least re-entered the parts I remember. If I leave now, my whole friggin' day will be a total write-off.
Ha ha! Well, I'm off. See ya!

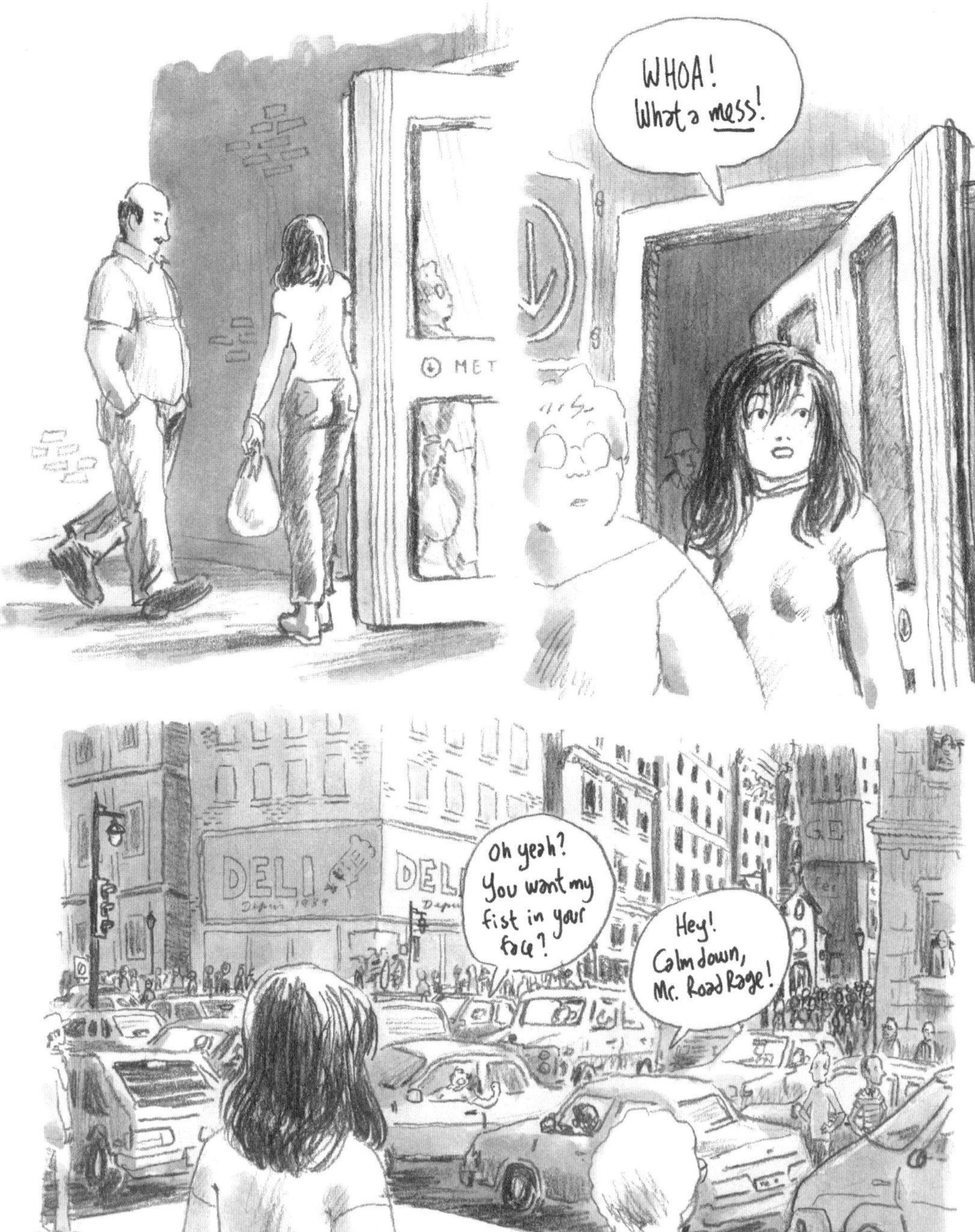
MET
WHOA! What a mess!
DELI
DELI
Oh yeah? You want my fist in your face?
Hey! Calm down, Mr. Road Rage!

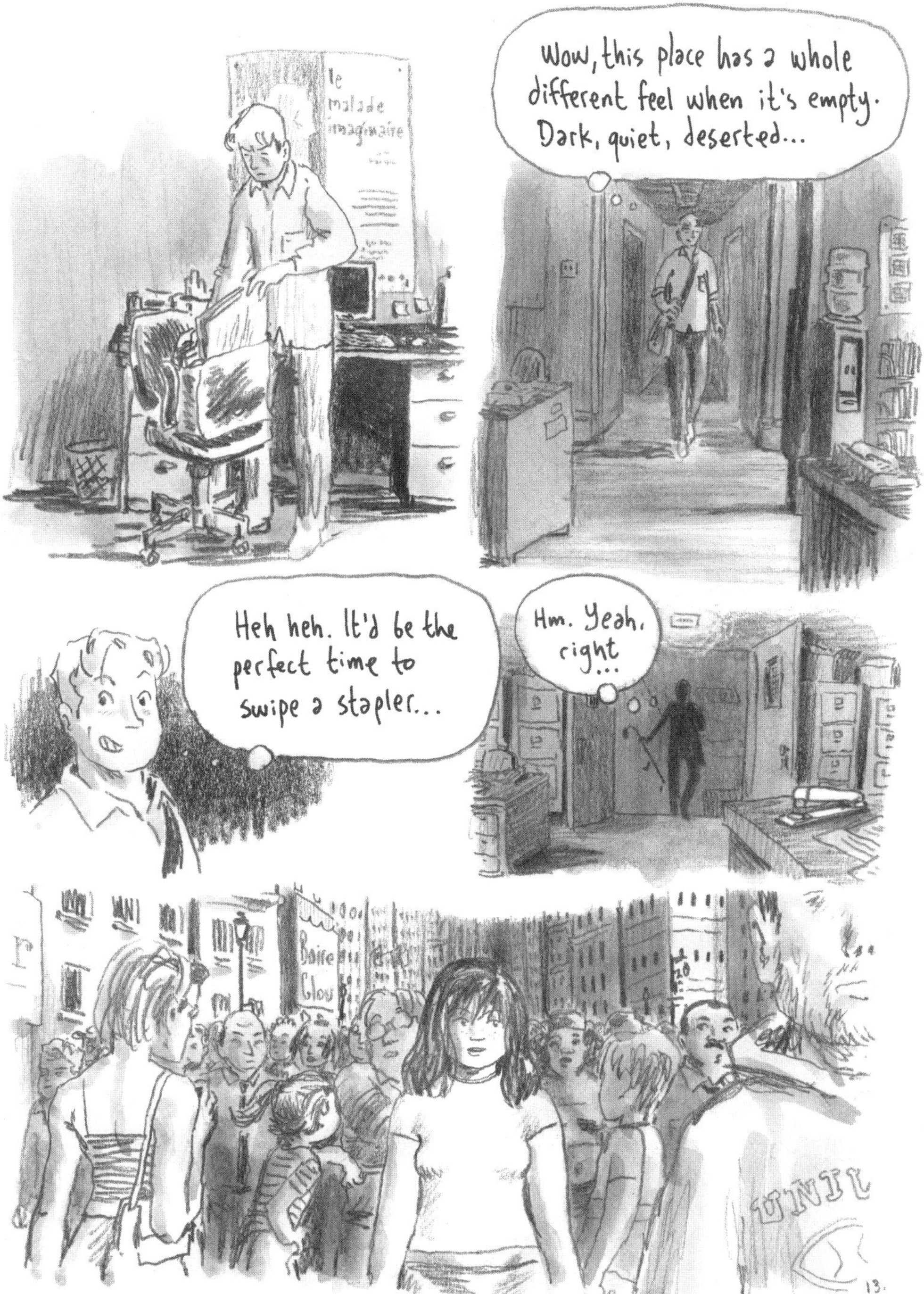
le malade imaginaire
Wow, this place has a whole different feel when it's empty. Dark, quiet, deserted...
Heh heh. It'd be the perfect time to swipe a stapler...
Hm. Yeah, right...

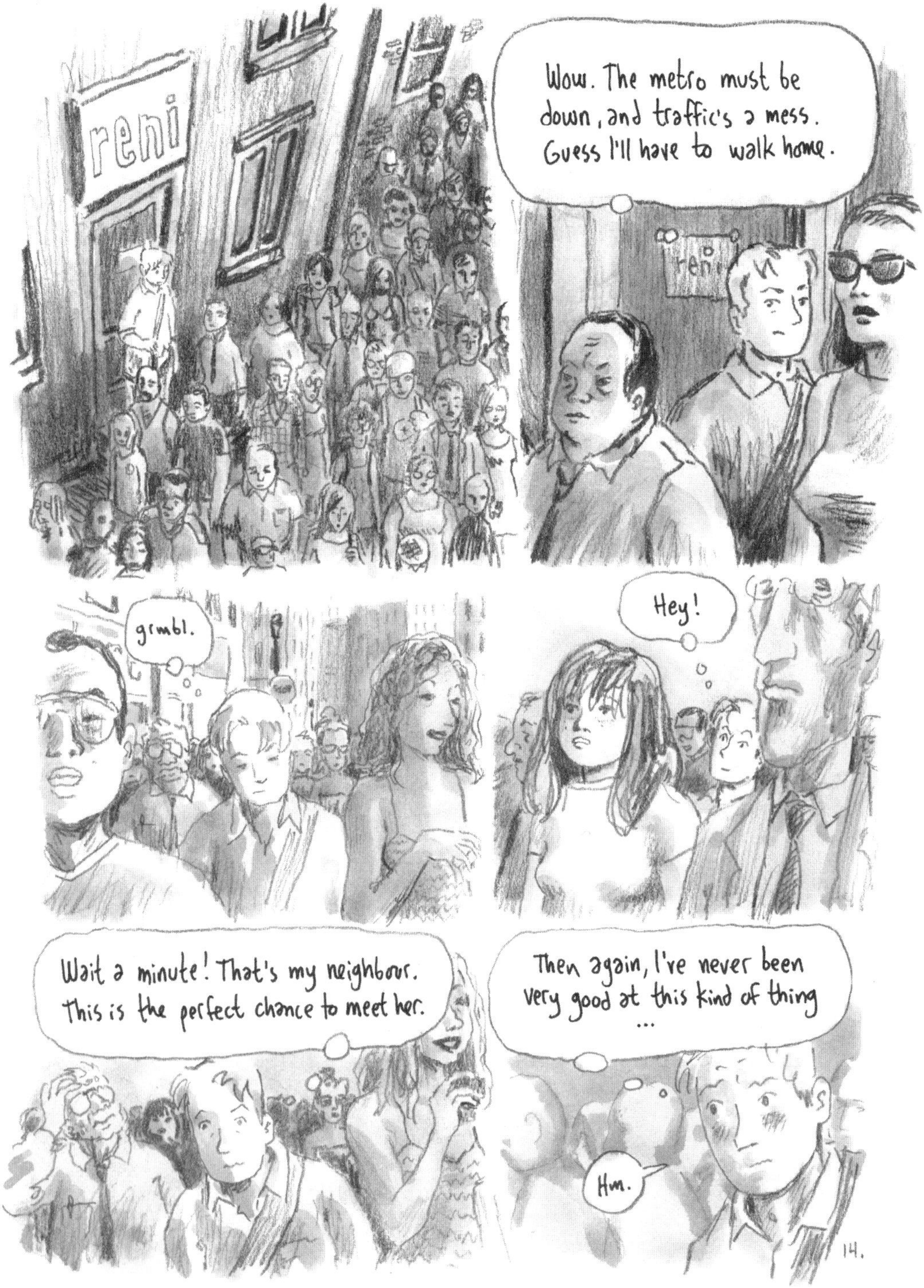

Wow. The metro must be down, and traffic's a mess. Guess I'll have to walk home.
grmbl.
Hey!
Wait a minute! That's my neighbour. This is the perfect chance to meet her.
Then again, I've never been very good at this kind of thing ...
Hm.

Ah, what the hell!
Uh... Excuse me?... Hello.
?
SHIT! Who is this guy?
Hello?
I'm not a creep, I'm not a rapist, I don't want your money, I don't mean any disrespect, I'm not some kind of jerk who's obsessed with hockey ...
Um ...
You don't recognize me? We're neighbours! I've seen you often at the store.
Oh!
Yup! I'm the bachelor next door!
No way! I did NOT just say that. How lame!

Ha! Ha... Ha.
Ho boy! We've got a real winner, here.
I'm such a moron!
Uh... my name's Simon.
Bernadette.
Pleasure.
Me too.
So! Bernadette. Nice name! So old-fashioned. Your friends must call you Bernie, do they?
Wow. Goofballs like this really do still exist. INCREDIBLE.
Oh my god. Way to go, Einstein. My life is over.

17.

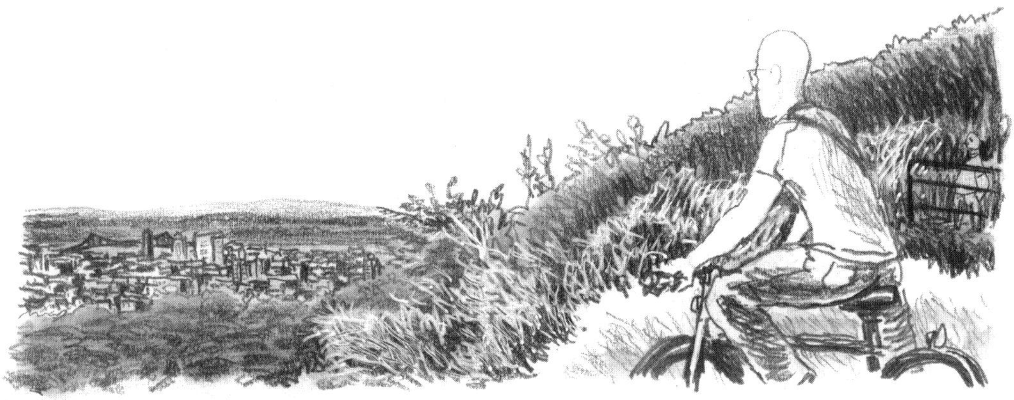

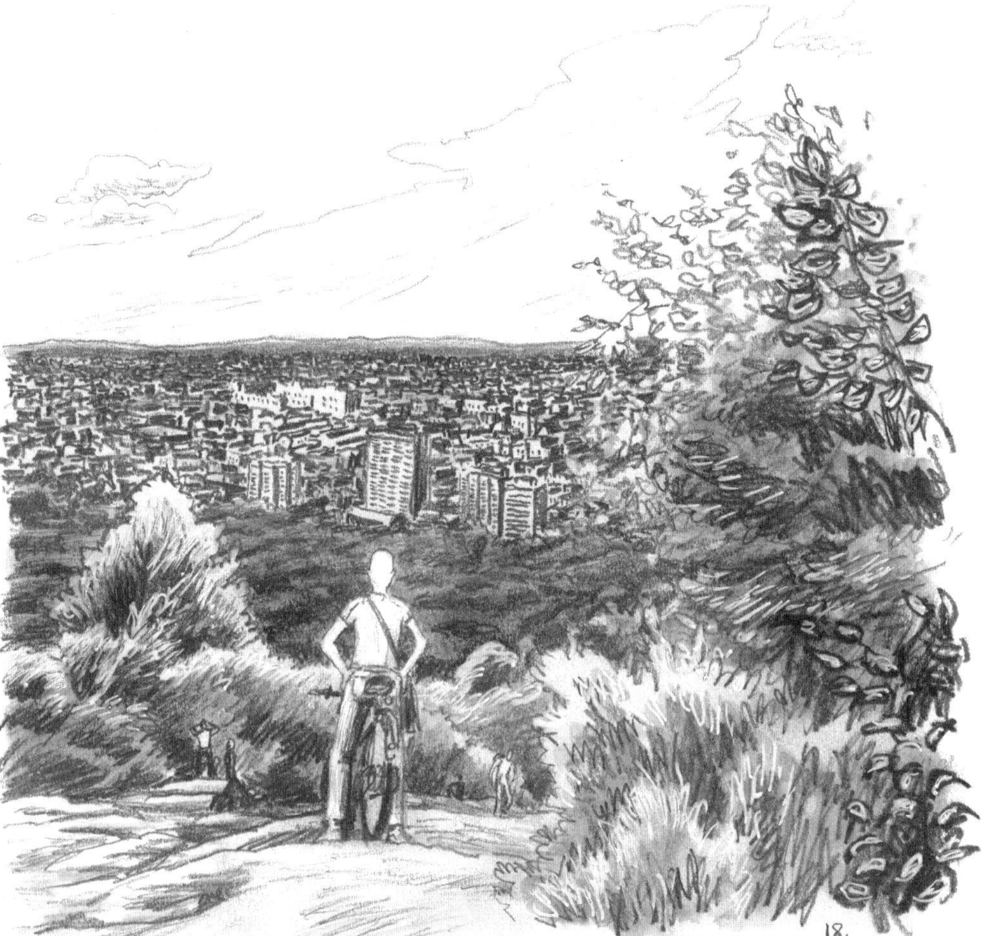

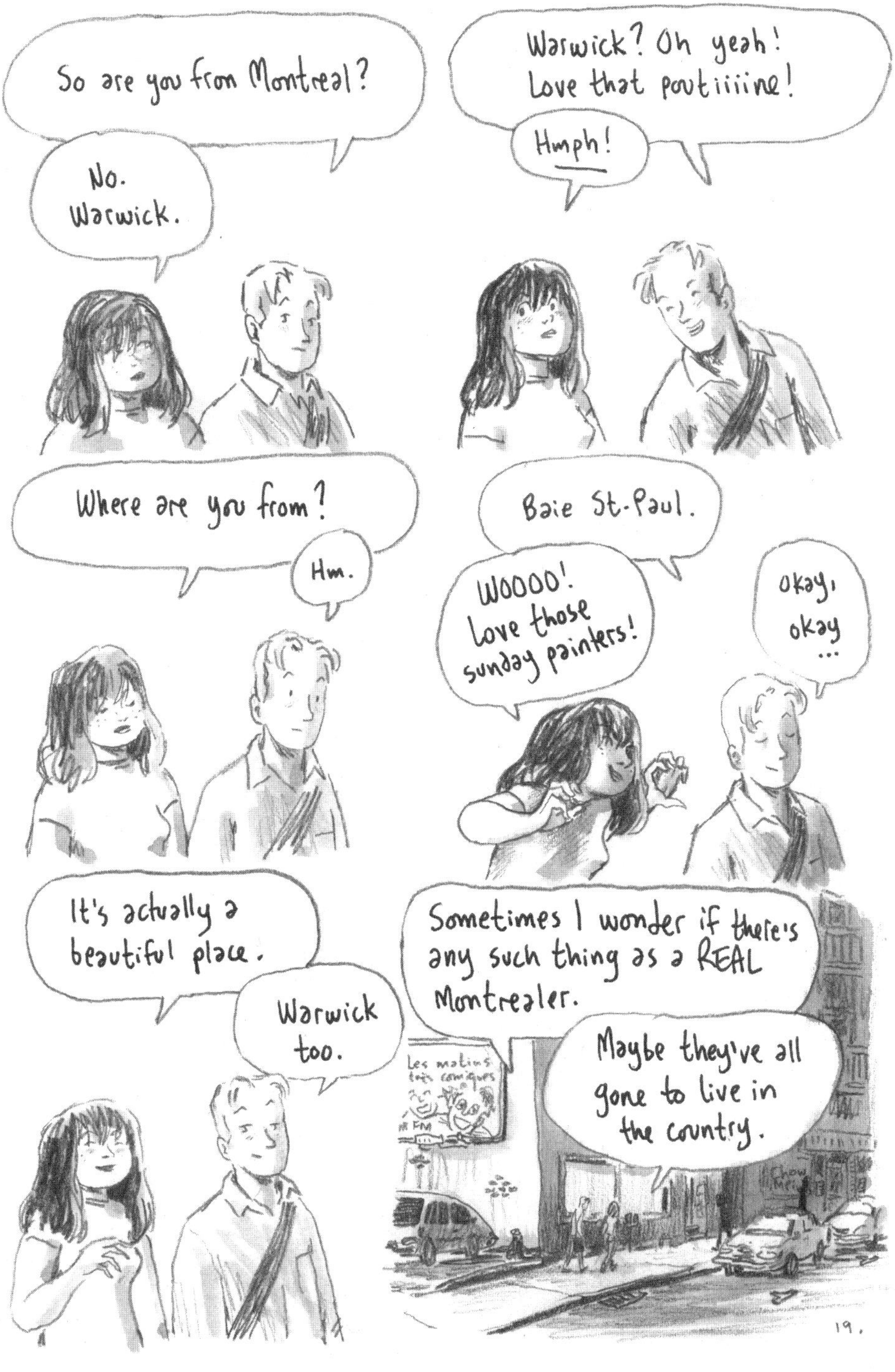
So are you from Montreal?
No. Warwick.
Warwick? Oh yeah! Love that poutiiiine!
Hmph!
Where are you from?
Hm.
Baie St-Paul.
WOOOO! Love those sunday painters!
okay, okay ...
It's actually a beautiful place.
Warwick too.
Sometimes I wonder if there's any such thing as a REAL Montrealer.
Maybe they've all gone to live in the country.
Les matins trop comiques
Chow Mein

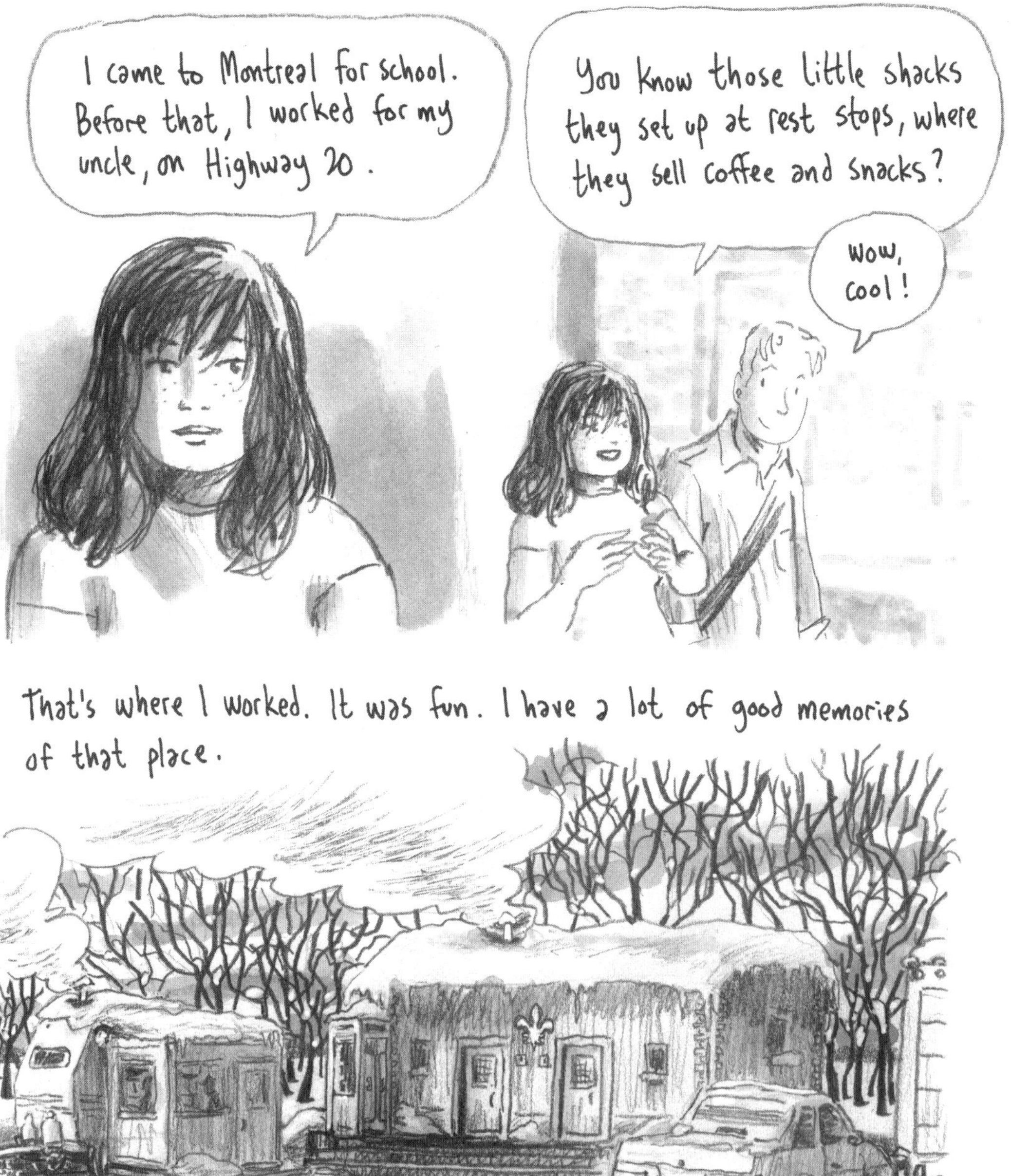
I came to Montreal for school. Before that, I worked for my uncle, on Highway 20.
You know those little shacks they set up at rest stops, where they sell coffee and snacks?
Wow, cool!
That's where I worked. It was fun. I have a lot of good memories of that place.

I enjoyed it. I was always meeting people who were on the go and almost hypnotized by the highway. I started at dawn; it was funny seeing so many complete strangers still half asleep.

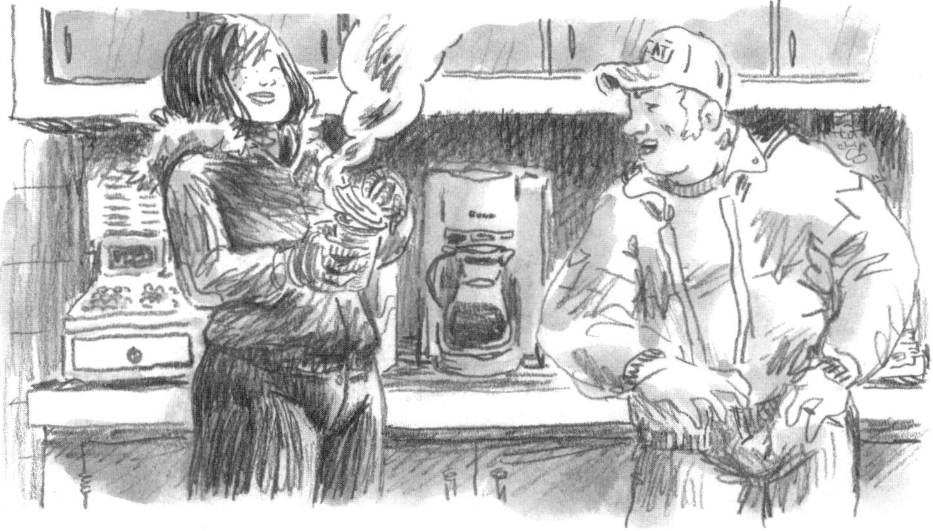

I definitely got to know all the truckers' jokes that year.

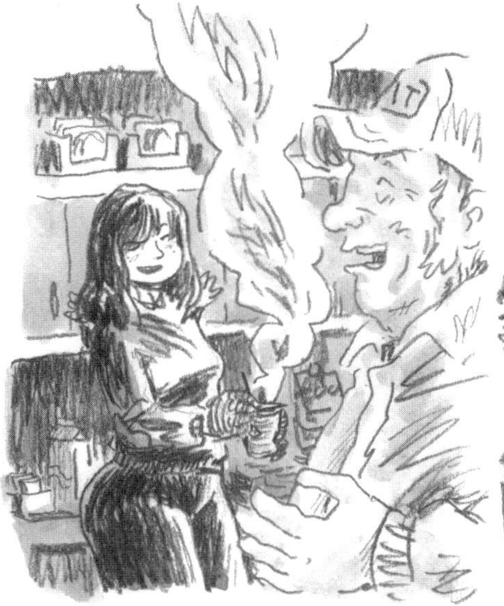

And then there were long periods of time when nobody came at all. All those endless afternoons. One thing's for sure: I'll never need to take a class in meditation.

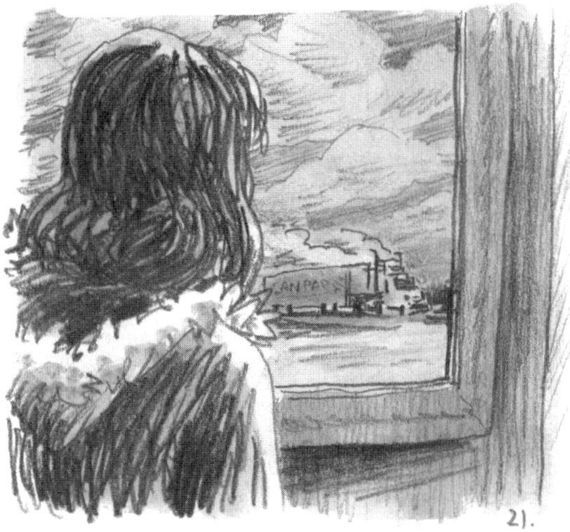

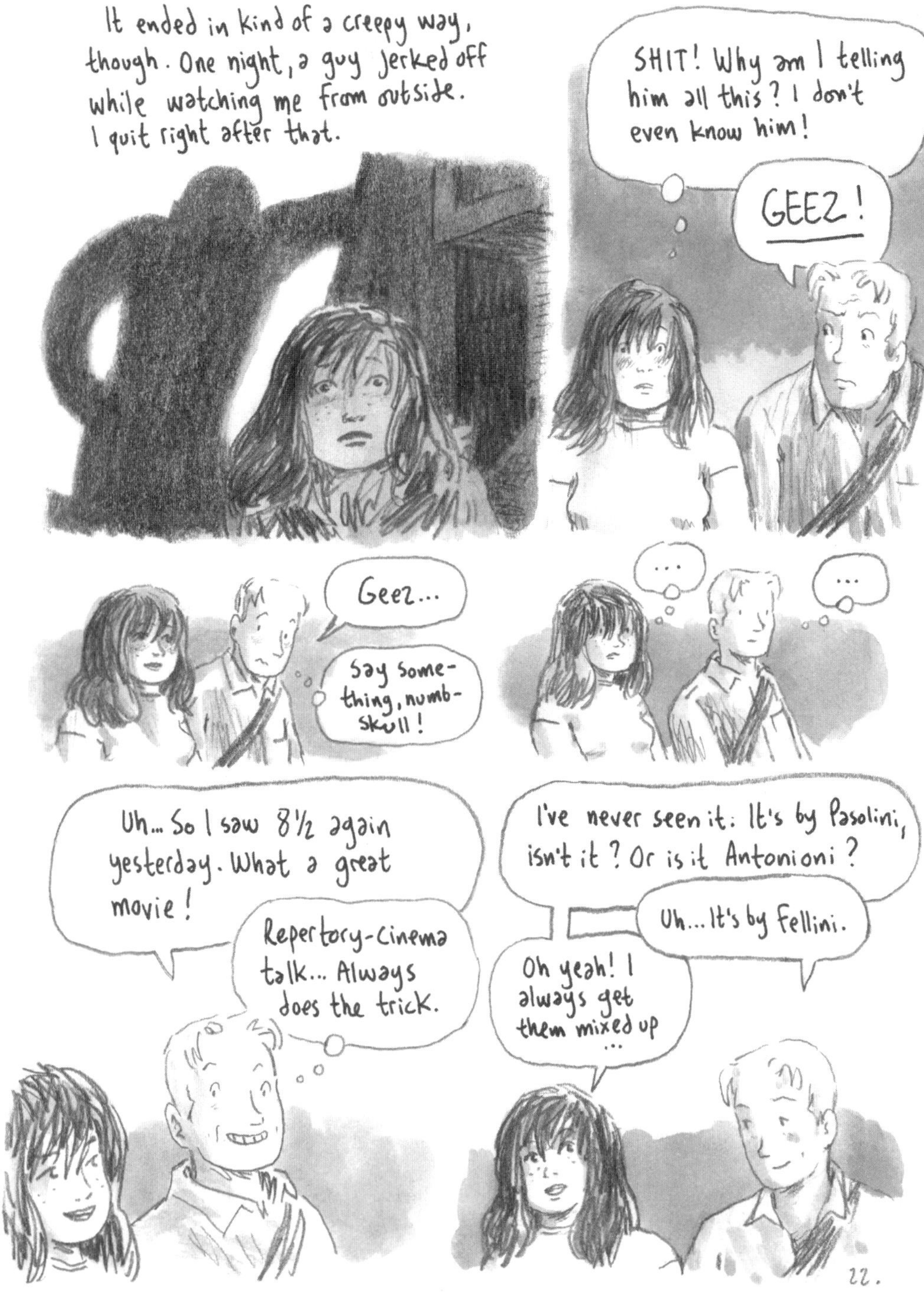
It ended in kind of a creepy way, though. One night, a guy jerked off while watching me from outside. I quit right after that.
SHIT! Why am I telling him all this? I don't even know him!
GEEZ!
Geez...
Say something, numbskull!
...
...
Uh... So I saw 8½ again yesterday. What a great movie!
Repertory-cinema talk... Always does the trick.
I've never seen it. It's by Pasolini, isn't it? Or is it Antonioni?
Uh... It's by Fellini.
Oh yeah! I always get them mixed up ...

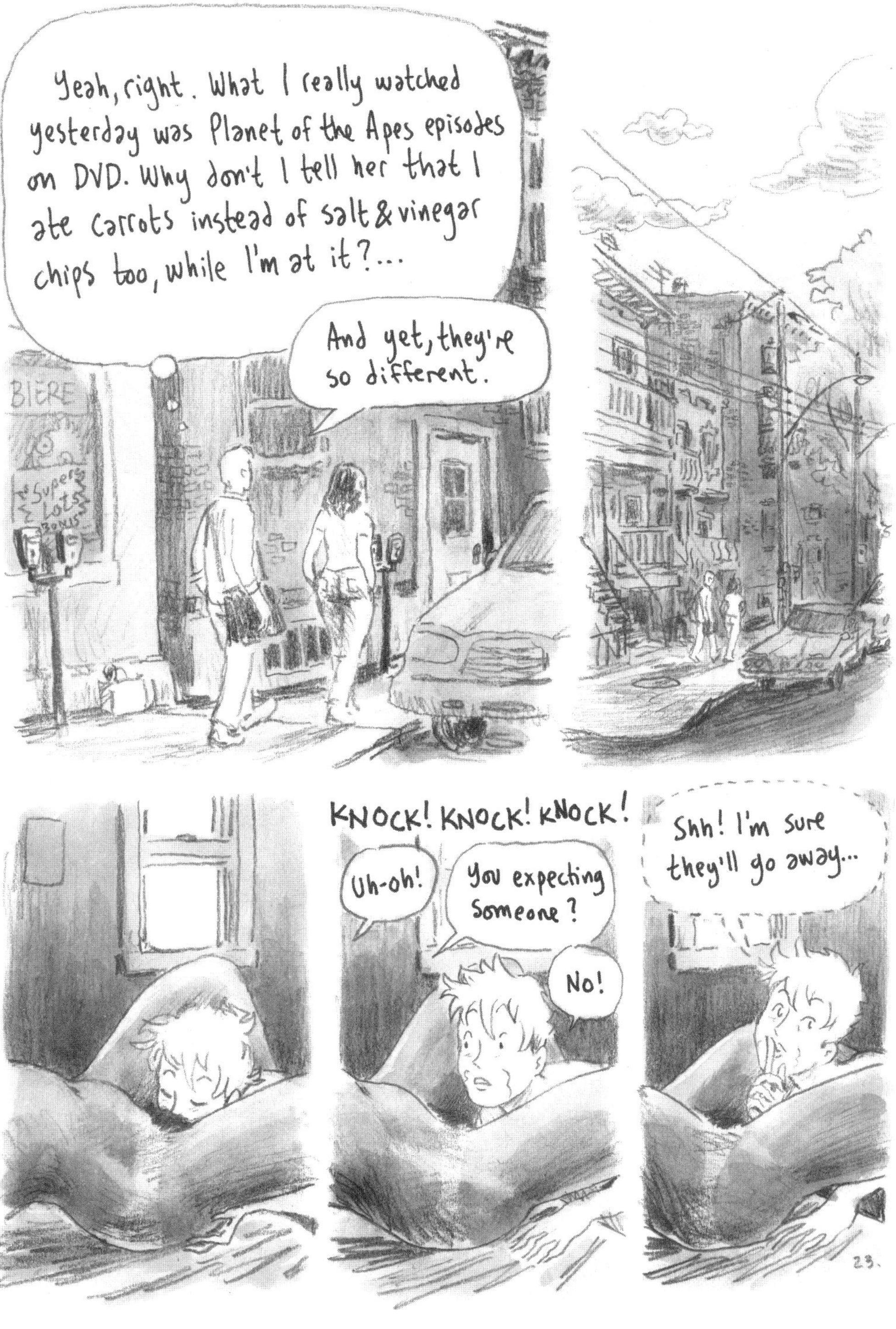
Yeah, right. What I really watched yesterday was Planet of the Apes episodes on DVD. Why don't I tell her that I ate carrots instead of salt & vinegar chips too, while I'm at it?...
And yet, they're so different.
BIÈRE
KNOCK! KNOCK! KNOCK!
Uh-oh!
You expecting someone?
No!
Shh! I'm sure they'll go away...

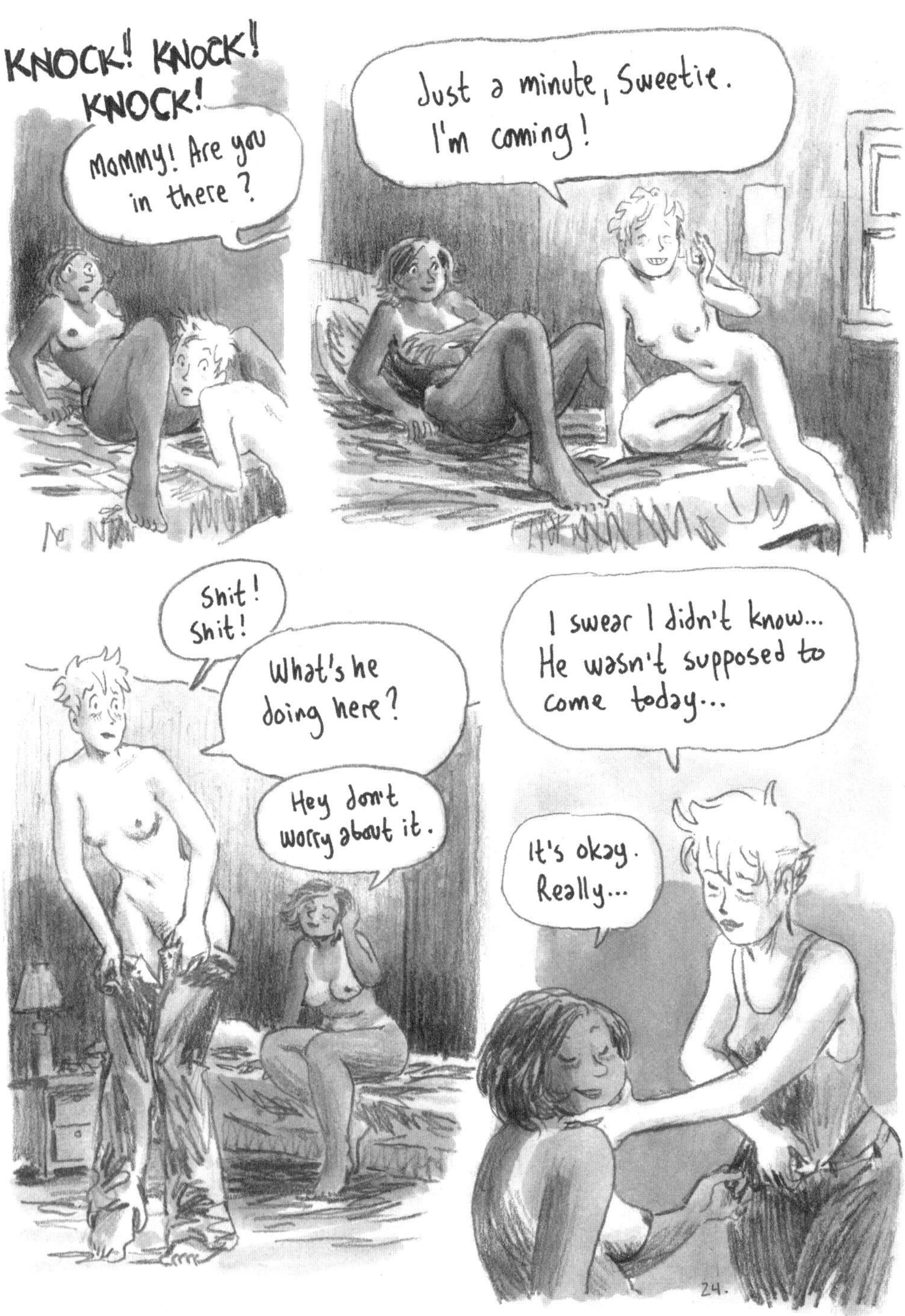
KNOCK! KNOCK! KNOCK!
Mommy! Are you in there ?
Just a minute, Sweetie. I'm coming!
Shit! Shit!
What's he doing here?
Hey don't worry about it.
I swear I didn't know... He wasn't supposed to come today...
It's okay. Really...

MOMMY! What're you doing?
Coming, Randall!
Hi, Sweethear... HMPF!
POW!
Hi... So... Can you take Randall for the rest of the day? I've got this thing...
Serge, it's your week. This is the third time you've done this to me!
Aw, come on!
snf. snf.
You smell funny.
Yay! Let's have fun! What can we do? What can we do?
uh...
clk.
25.

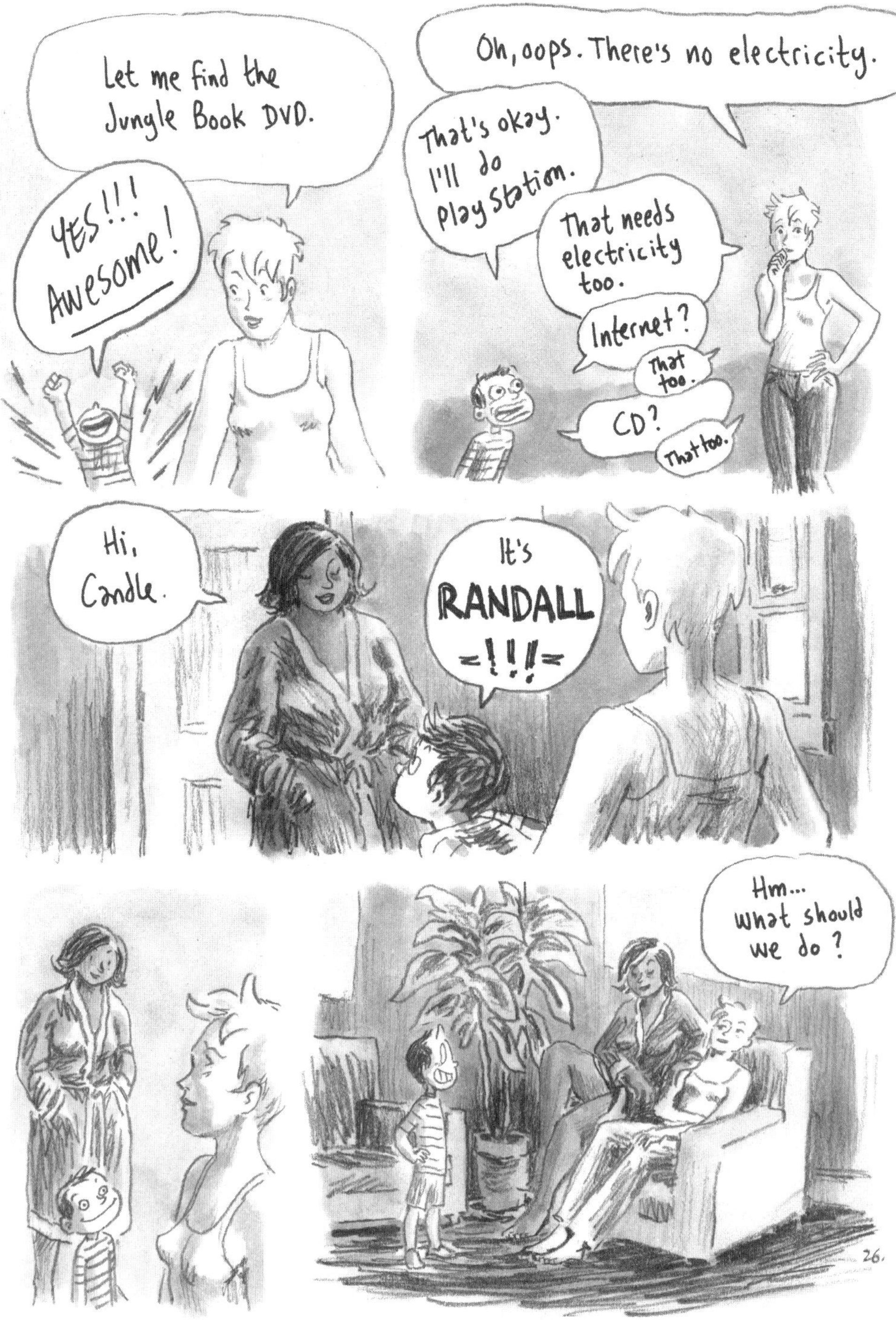

Let me find the Jungle Book DVD.
YES!!! Awesome!
Oh, oops. There's no electricity.
That's okay. I'll do PlayStation.
That needs electricity too.
Internet?
That too.
CD?
That too.
Hi, Candle.
It's RANDALL =!!!=
Hm... what should we do?

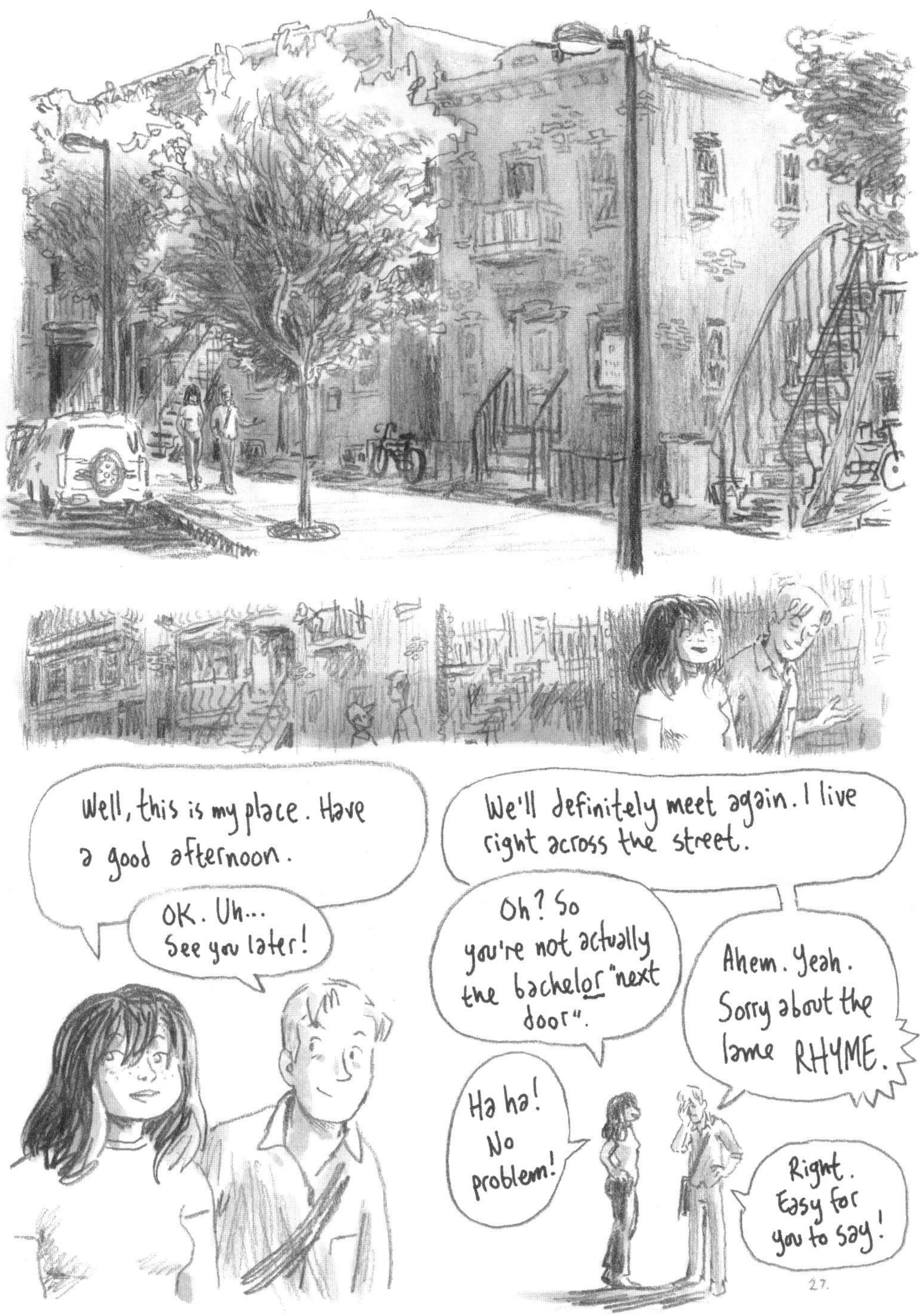
Well, this is my place. Have a good afternoon.
OK. Uh... See you later!
We'll definitely meet again. I live right across the street.
Oh? So you're not actually the bachelor "next door".
Ahem. Yeah. Sorry about the lame RHYME.
Ha ha! No problem!
Right. Easy for you to say!

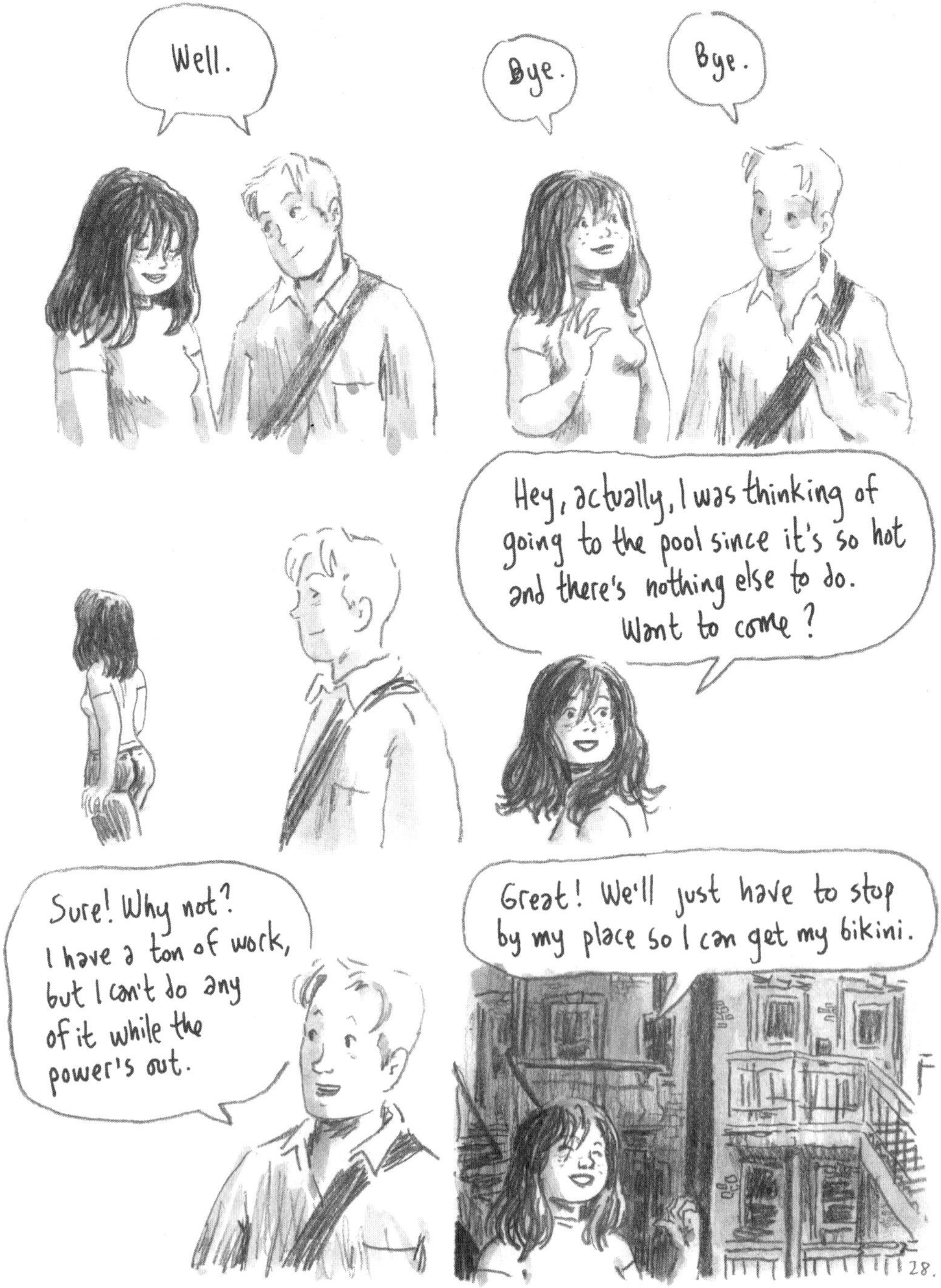

Well.
Bye.
Bye.
Hey, actually, I was thinking of going to the pool since it's so hot and there's nothing else to do. Want to come?
Sure! Why not? I have a ton of work, but I can't do any of it while the power's out.
Great! We'll just have to stop by my place so I can get my bikini.

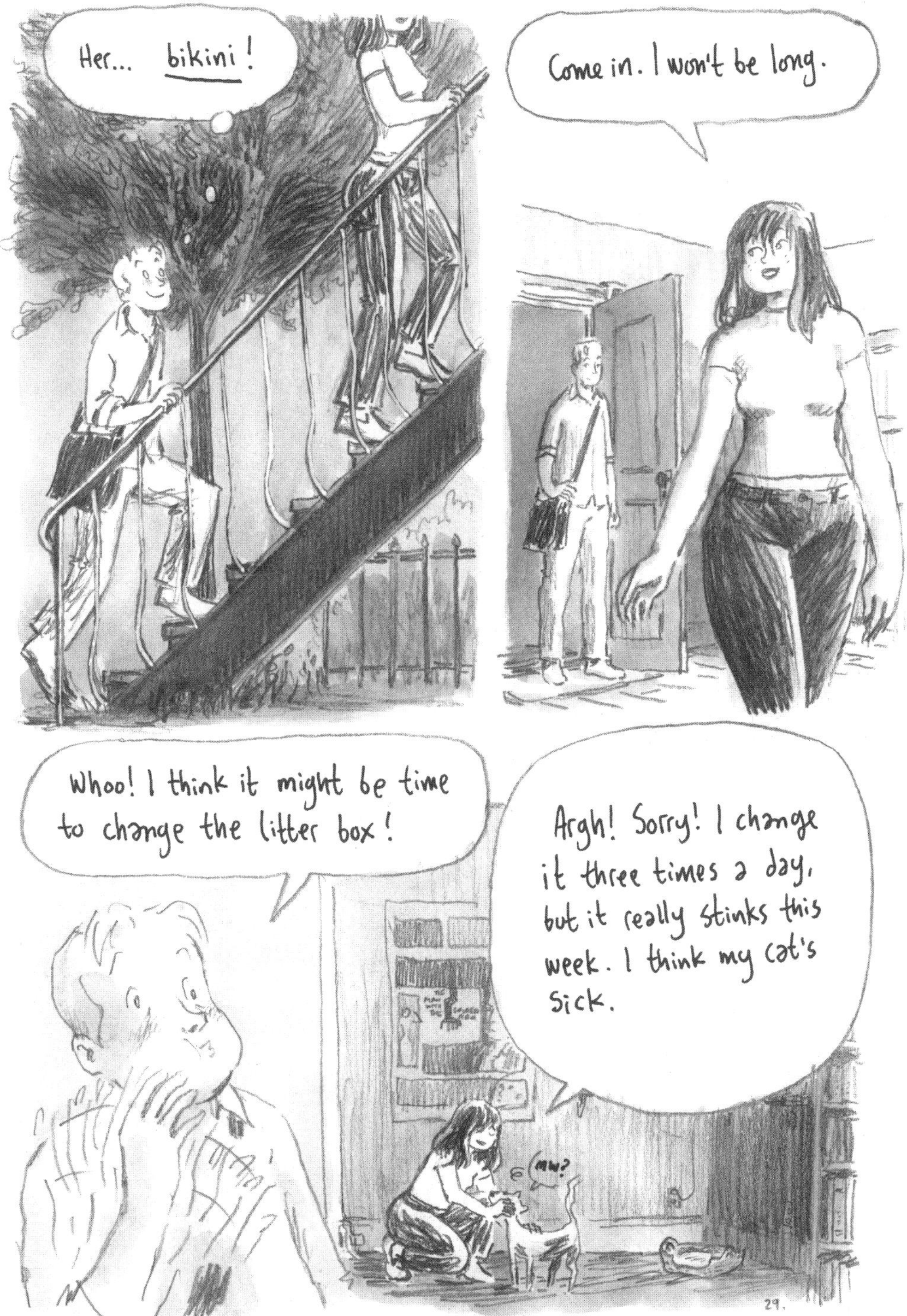
Her... bikini!
Come in. I won't be long.
Whoo! I think it might be time to change the litter box!
Argh! Sorry! I change it three times a day, but it really stinks this week. I think my cat's sick.
mw?

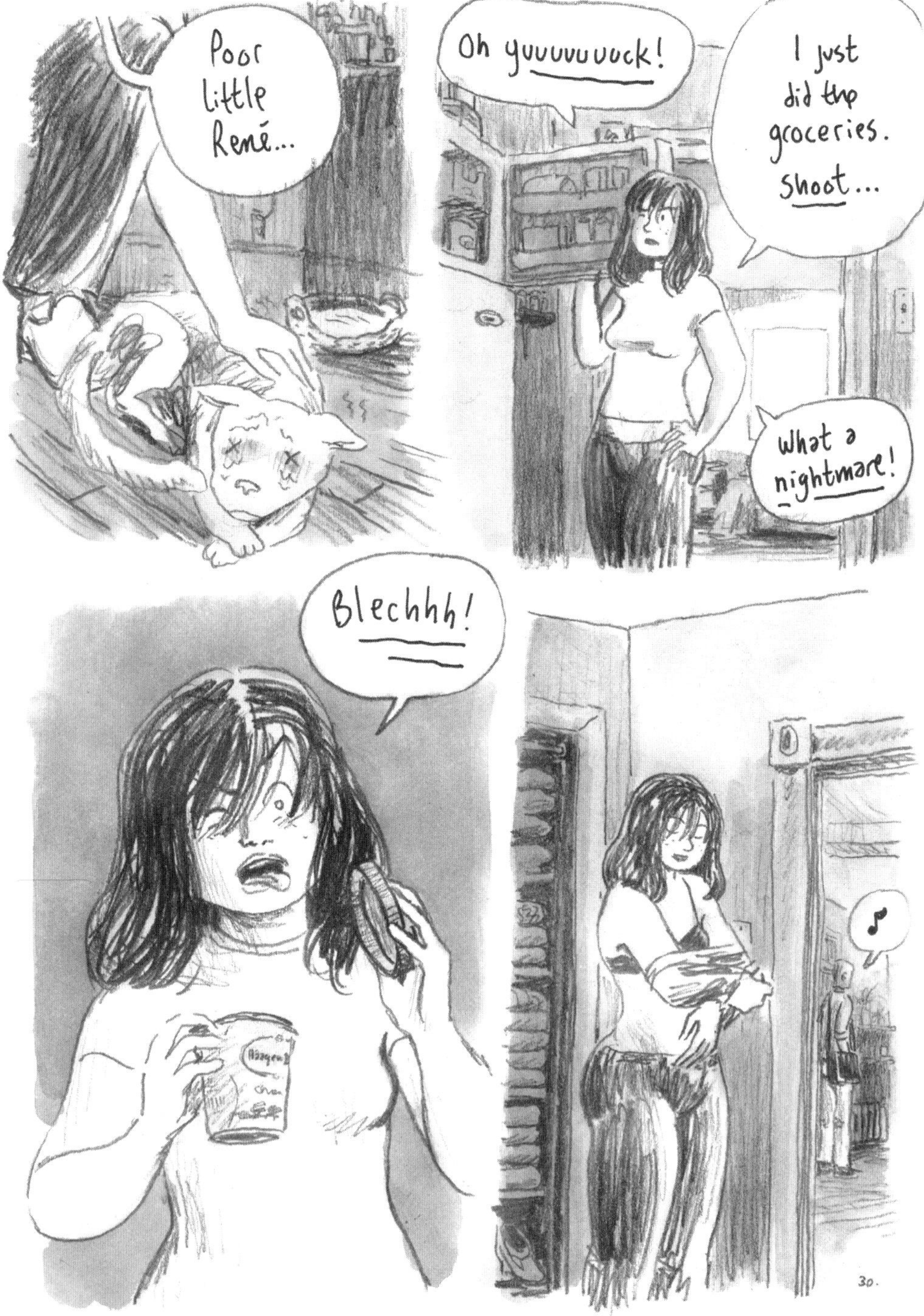
Poor little René...
Oh yuuuuuuck!
I just did the groceries. Shoot...
What a nightmare!
Blechhh!

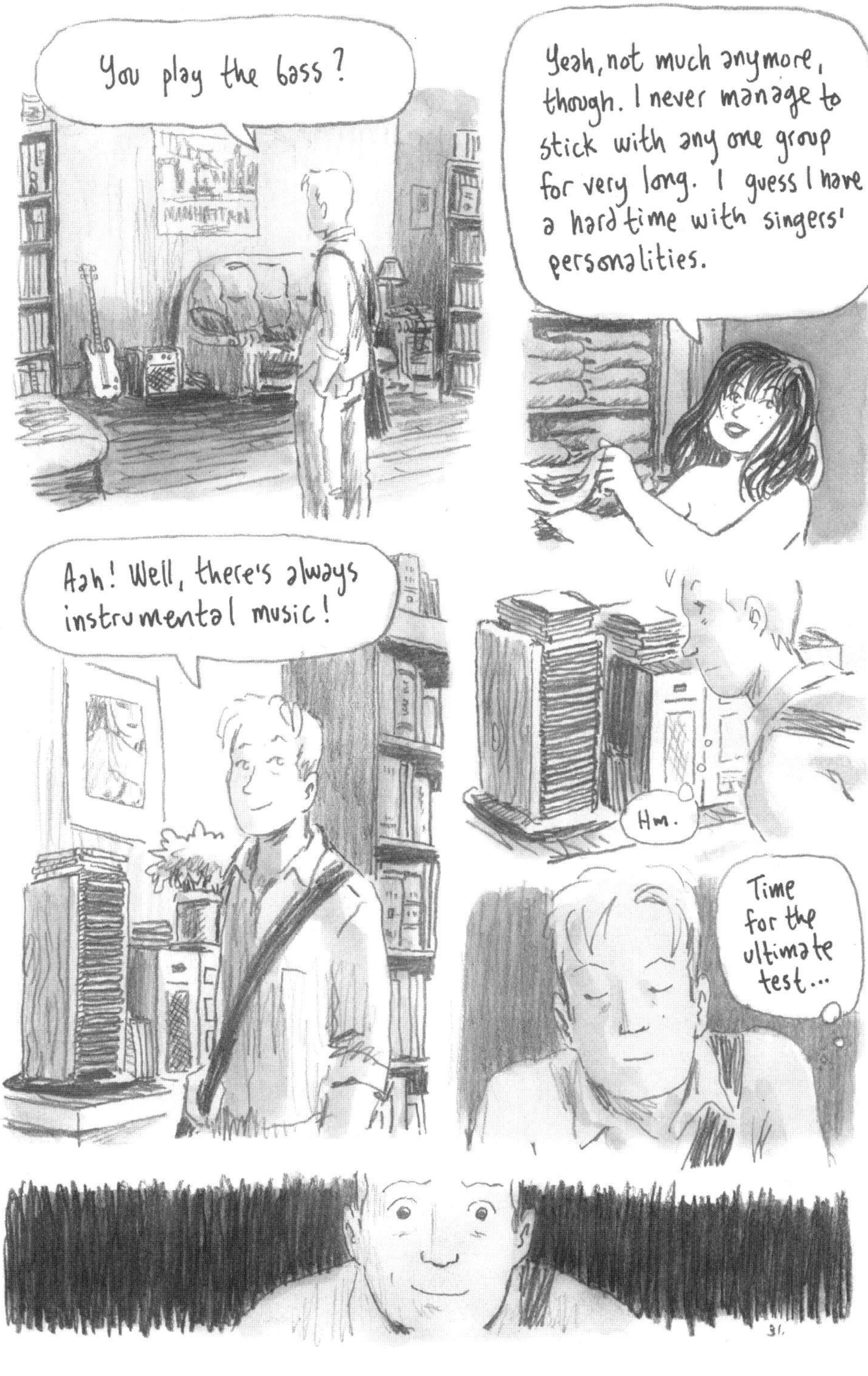
You play the bass?
Yeah, not much anymore, though. I never manage to stick with any one group for very long. I guess I have a hard time with singers' personalities.
Aah! Well, there's always instrumental music!
Hm.
Time for the ultimate test...

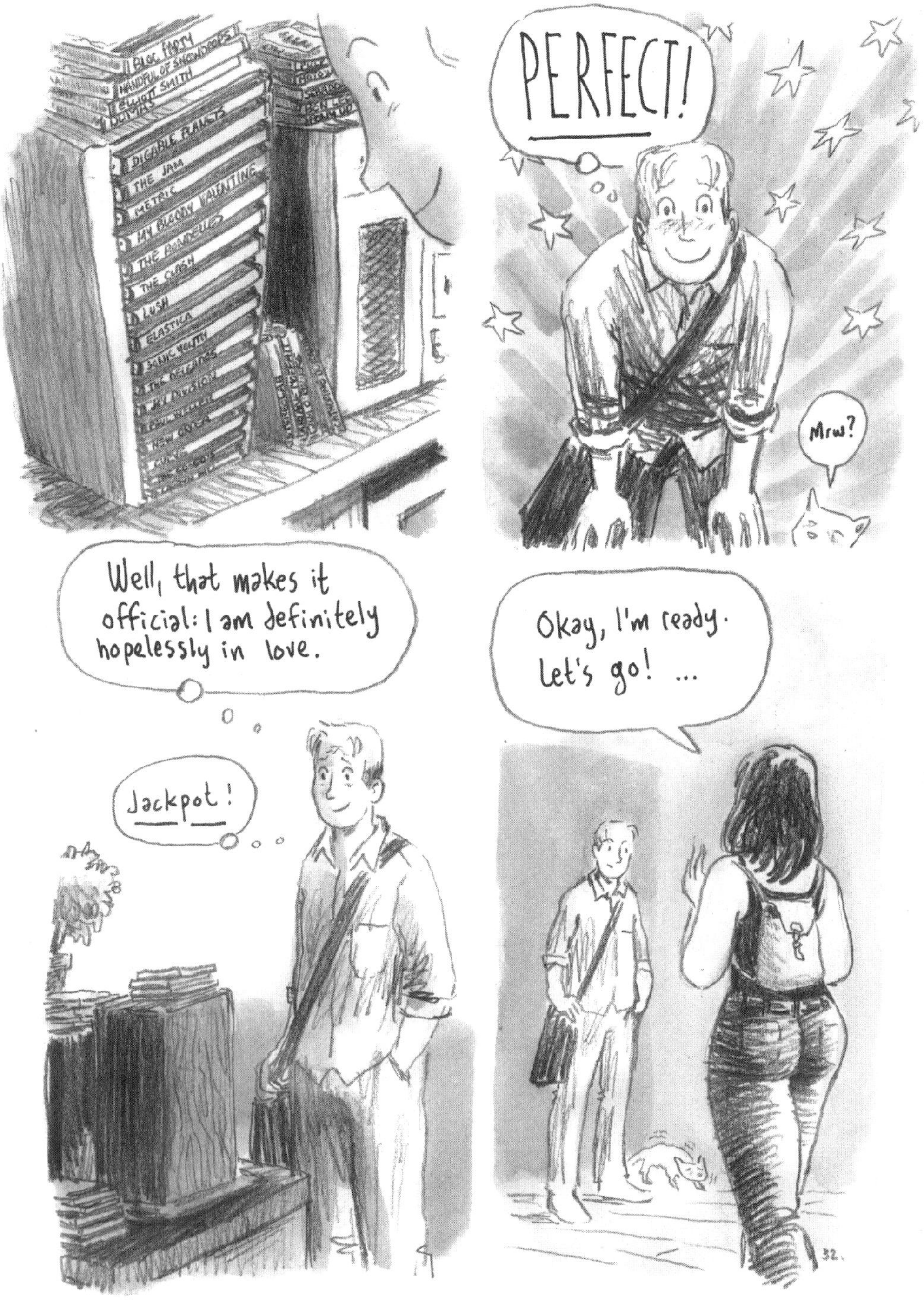
BLOC PARTY
HANDFUL OF SNOWDROPS
ELLIOTT SMITH
DIGABLE PLANETS
THE JAM
METRIC
MY BLOODY VALENTINE
THE RONDELLES
THE CLASH
LUSH
ELASTICA
PERFECT!
Mrw?
Well, that makes it official: I am definitely hopelessly in love.
Jackpot!
Okay, I'm ready. Let's go! ...

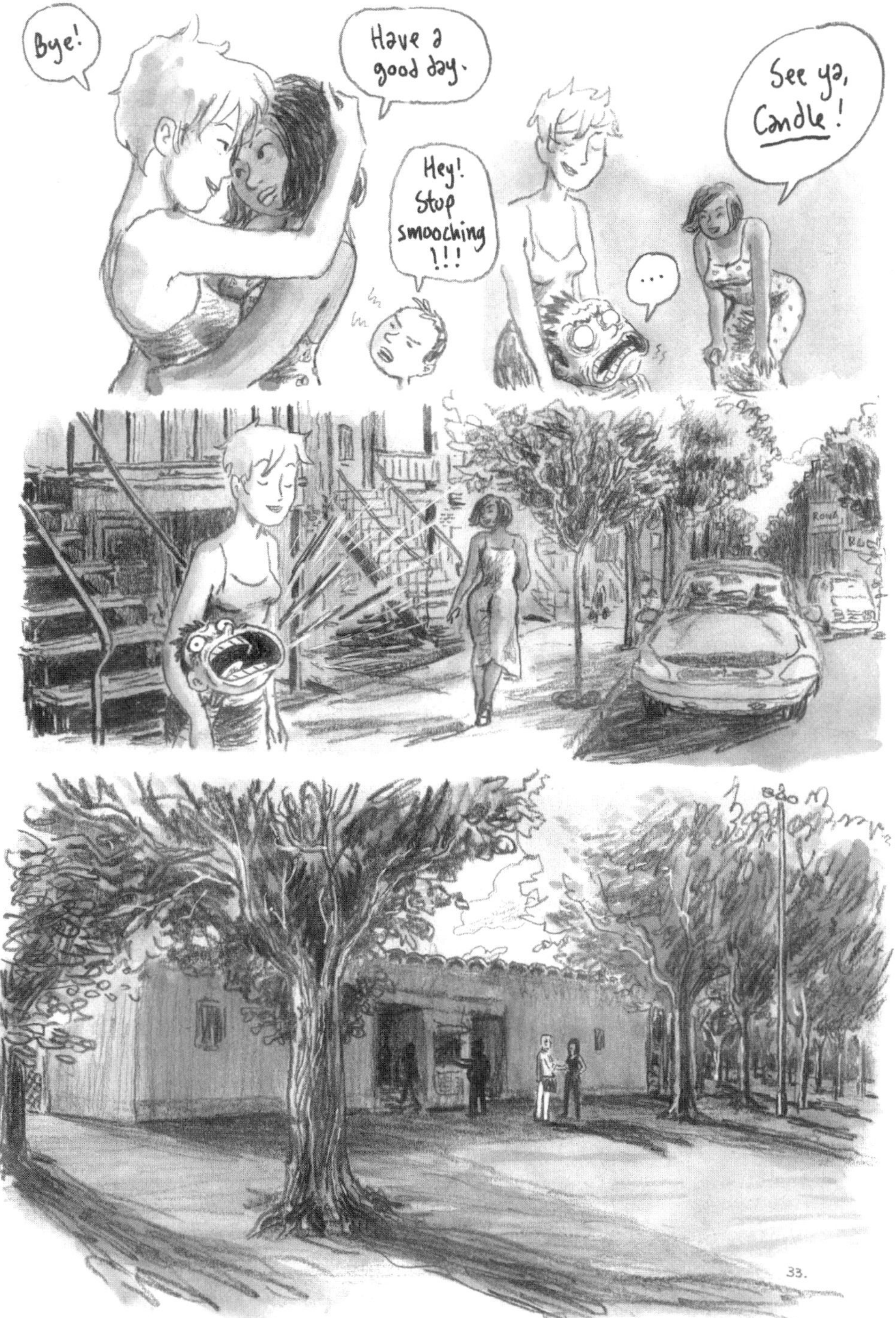
Bye!
Have a good day.
Hey! Stop smooching !!!
...
See ya, Candle!

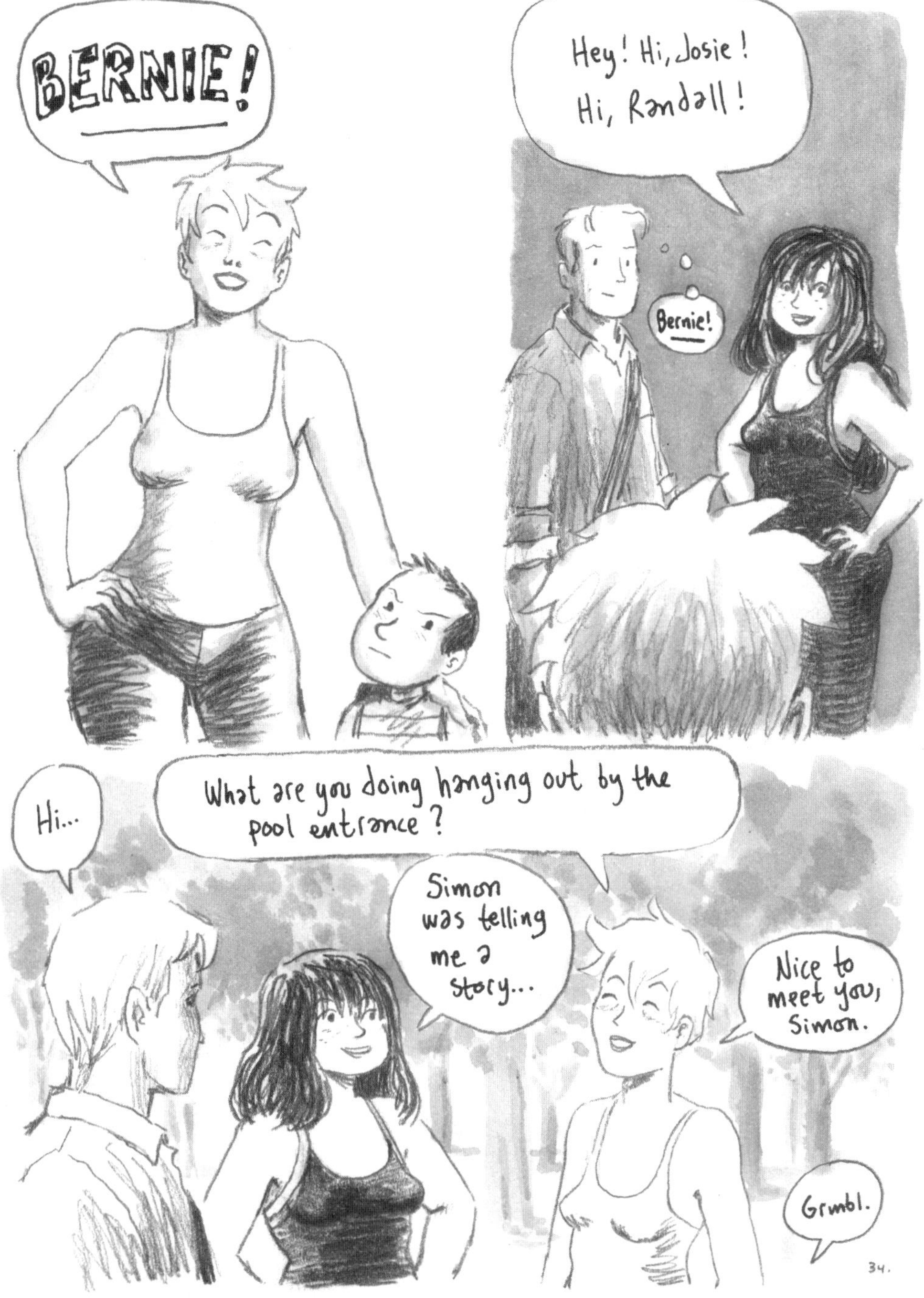
BERNIE!
Hey! Hi, Josie! Hi, Randall!
Bernie!
Hi...
What are you doing hanging out by the pool entrance?
Simon was telling me a story...
Nice to meet you, Simon.
Grmbl.

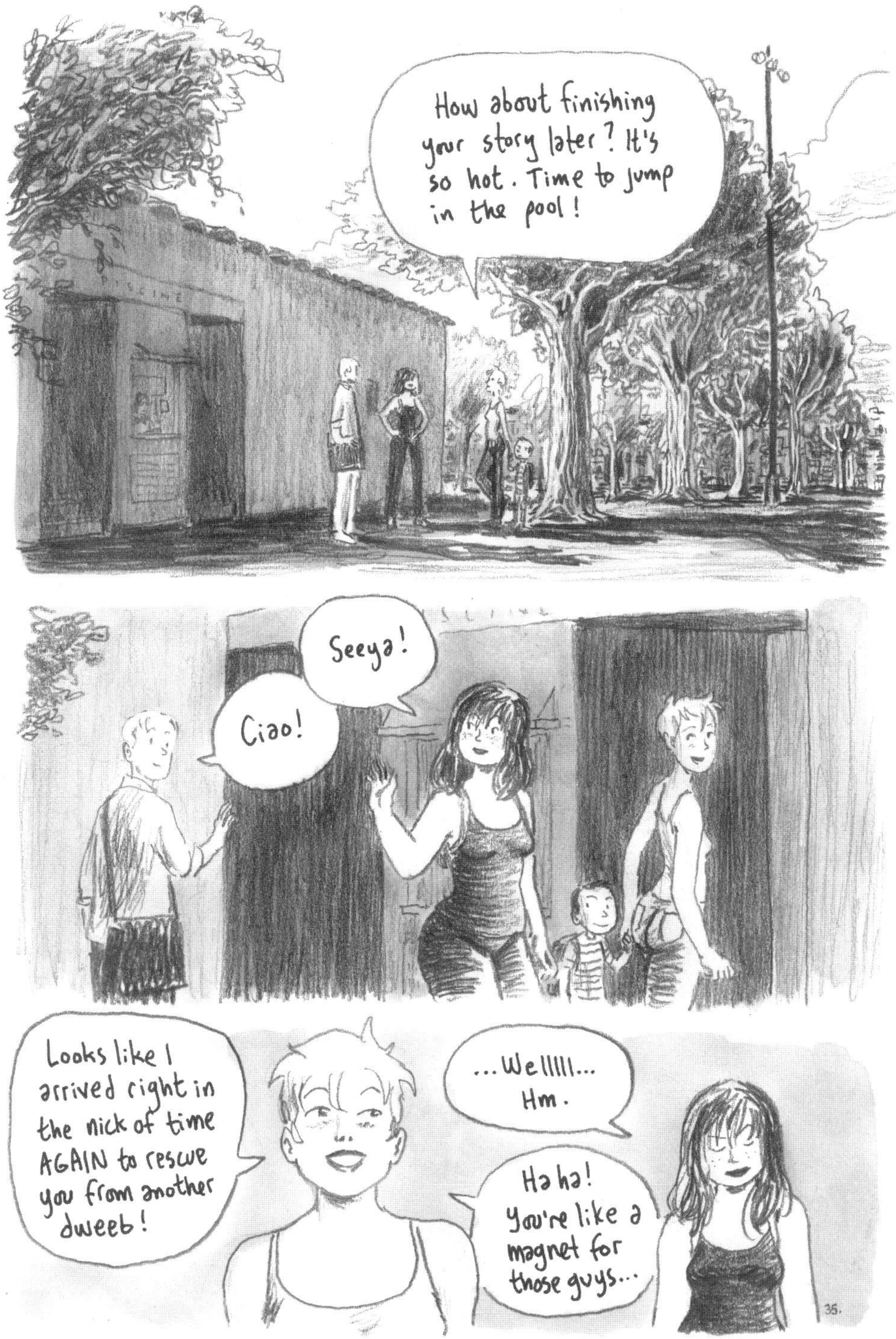
How about finishing your story later? It's so hot. Time to jump in the pool!
Seeya!
Ciao!
Looks like I arrived right in the nick of time AGAIN to rescue you from another dweeb!
...Welllll... Hm.
Ha ha! You're like a magnet for those guys...

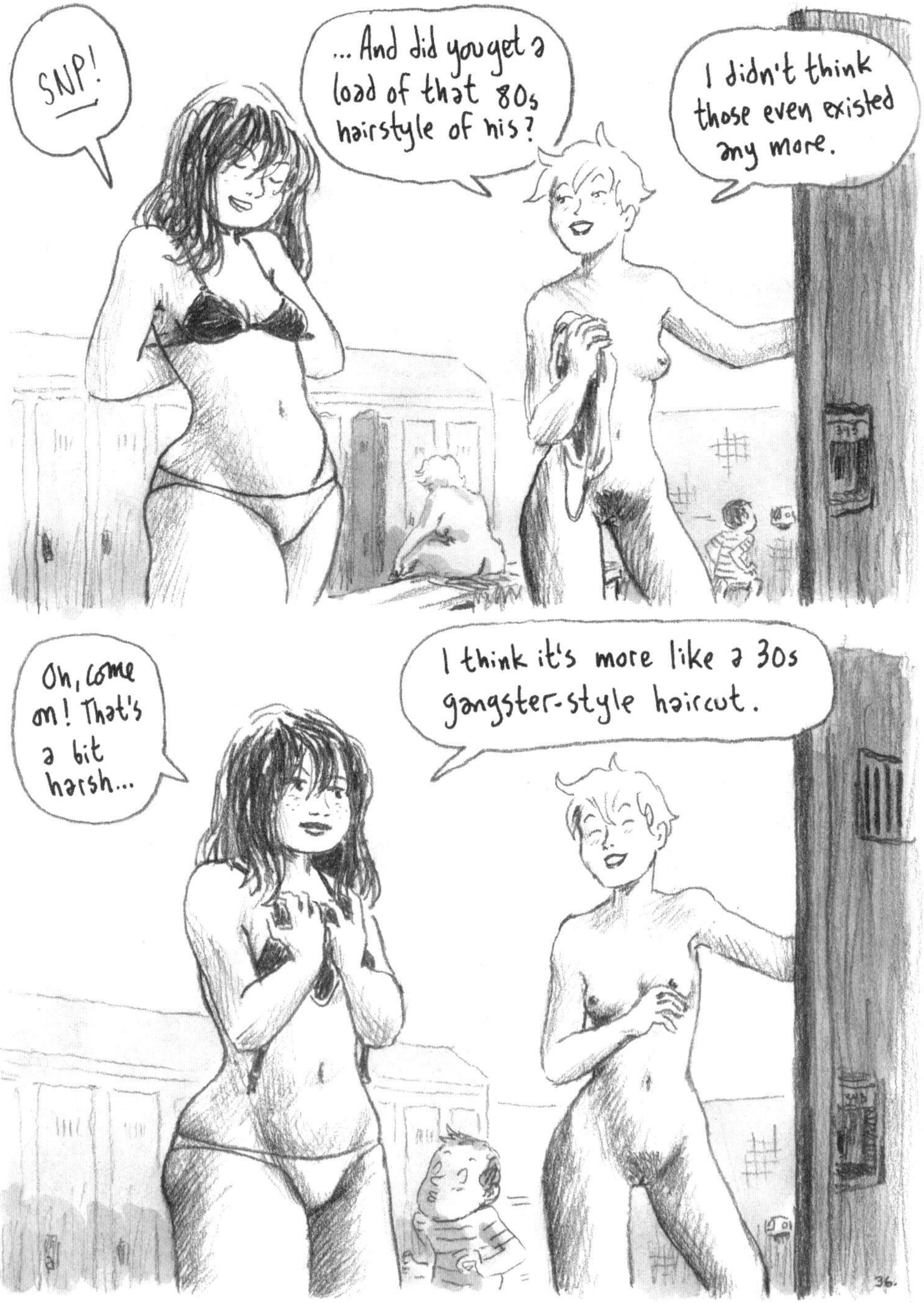
SNP!
... And did you get a load of that 80s hairstyle of his?
I didn't think those even existed any more.
Oh, come on! That's a bit harsh...
I think it's more like a 30s gangster-style haircut.
36.

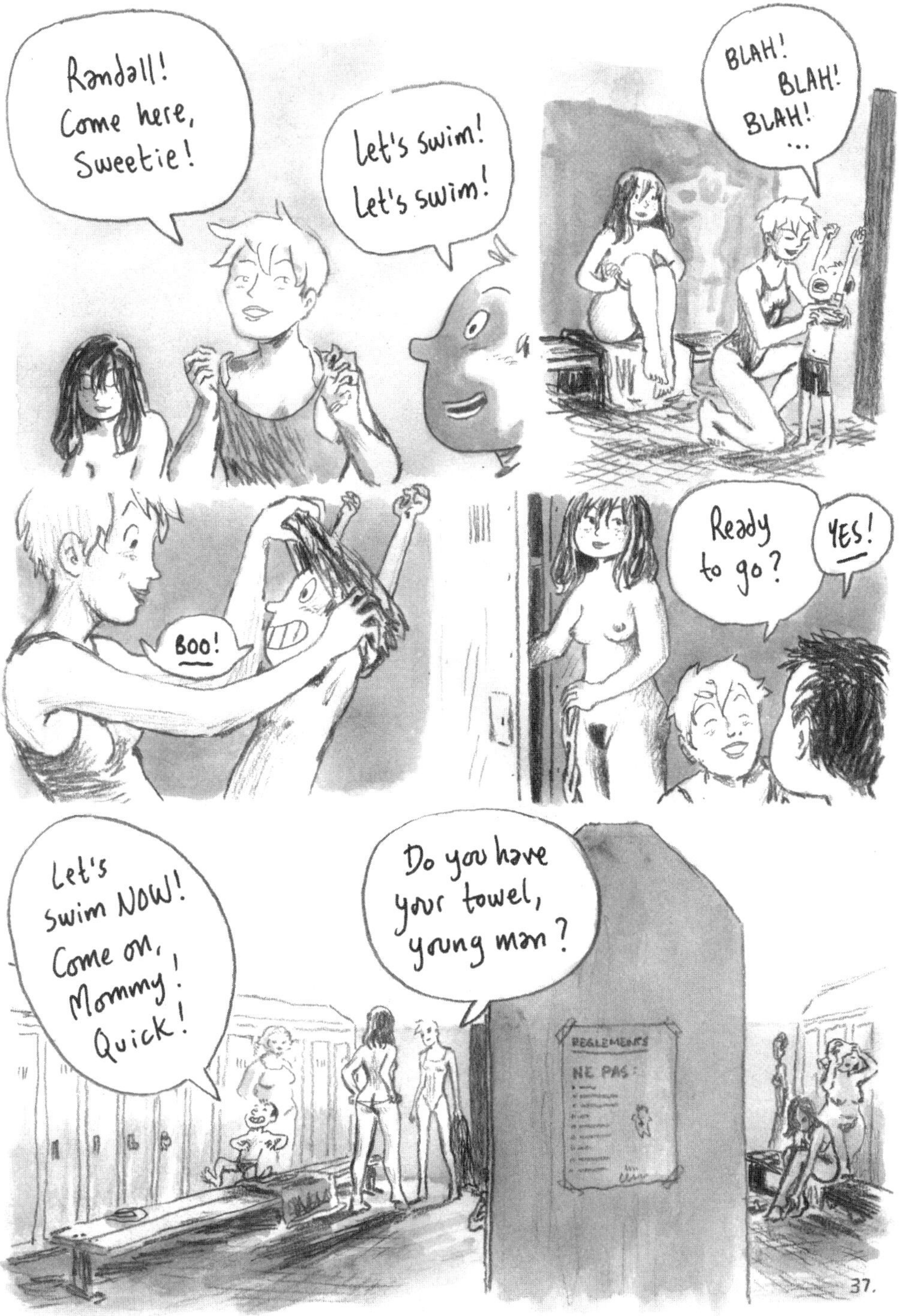
Randall! Come here, Sweetie!
Let's swim! Let's swim!
BLAH! BLAH! BLAH! ...
BOO!
Ready to go?
YES!
Let's swim NOW! Come on, Mommy! Quick!
Do you have your towel, young man?
REGLEMENTS
NE PAS :

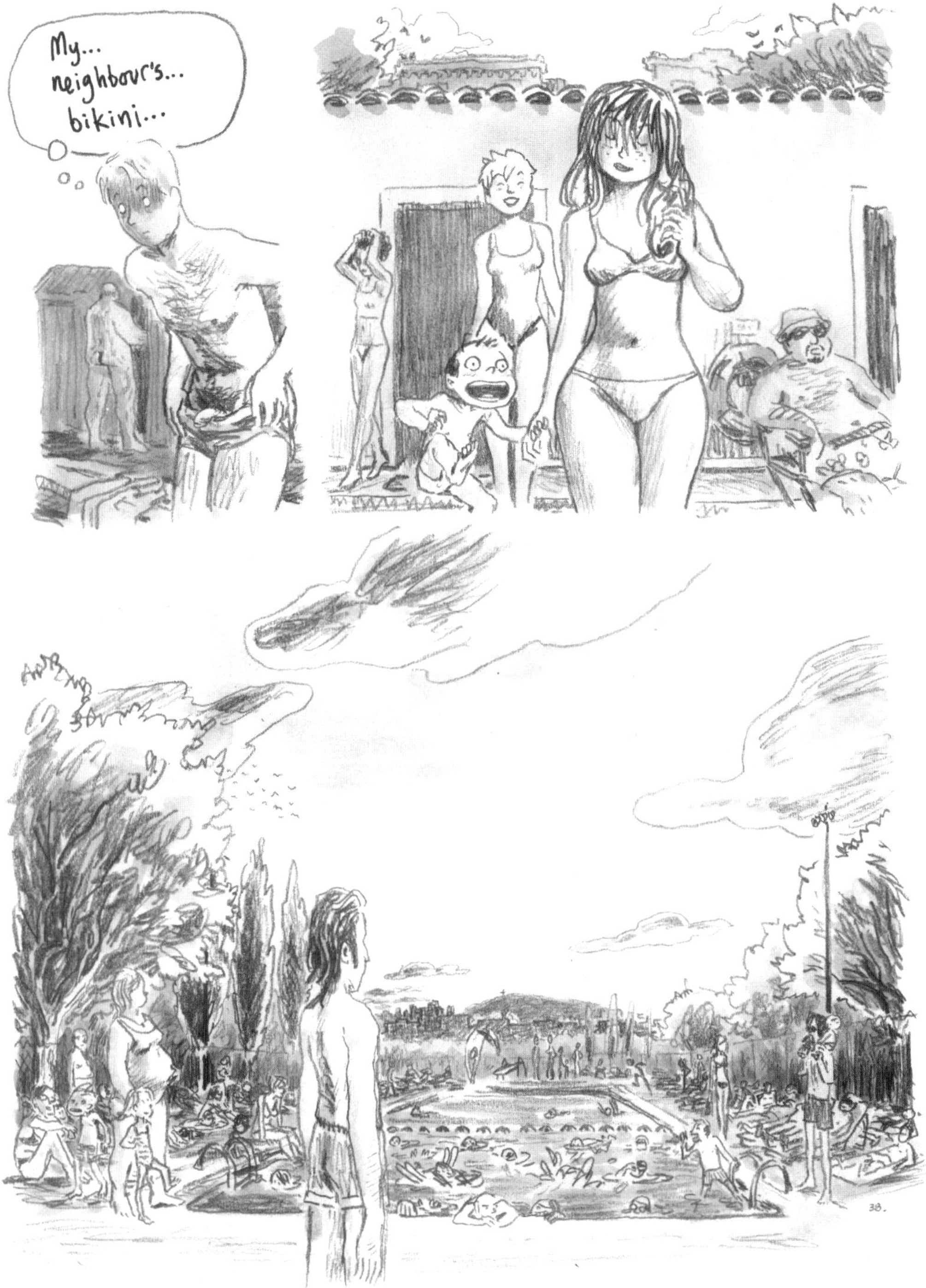
My... neighbour's... bikini...

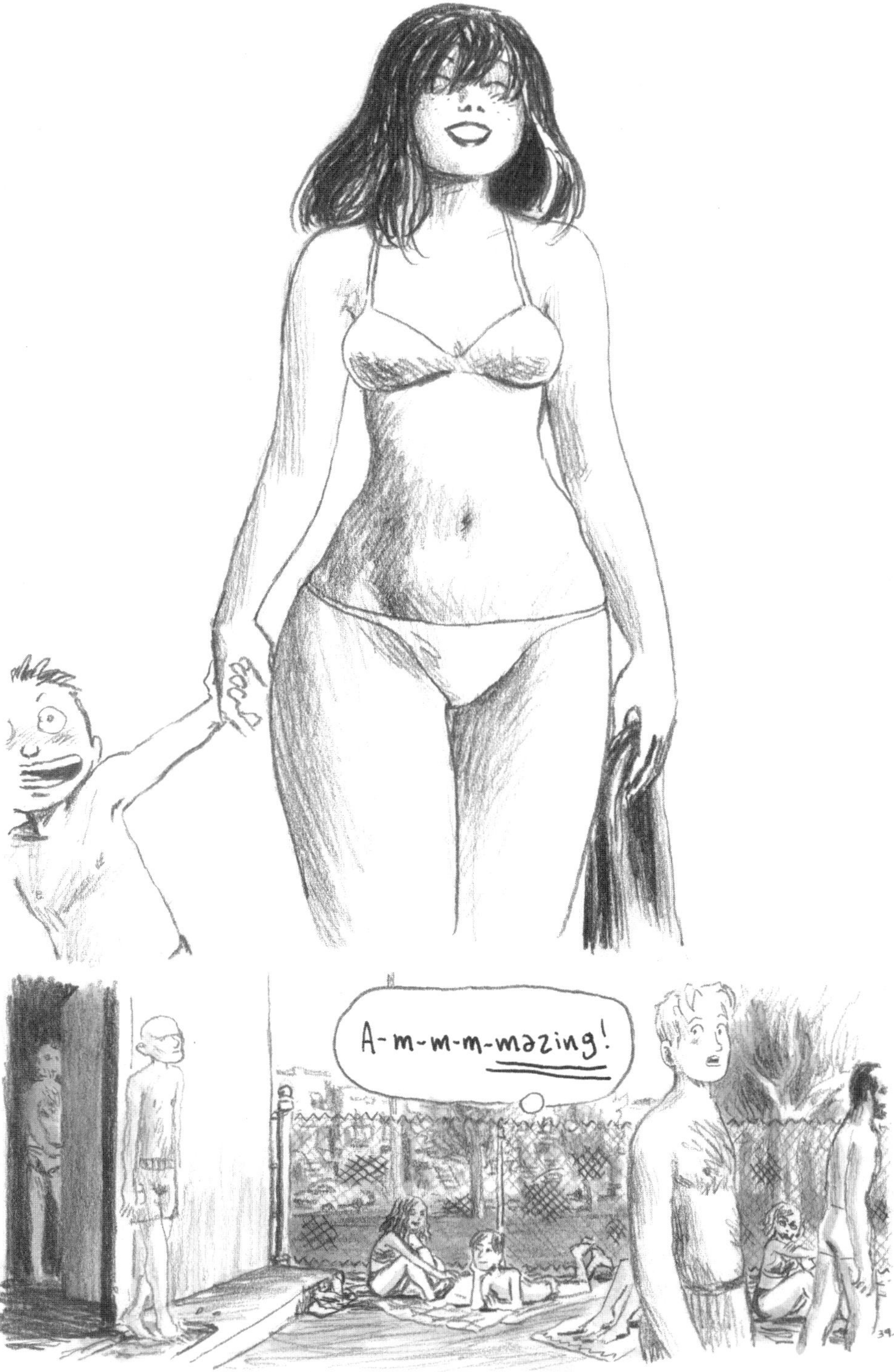
A-m-m-m-mazing!

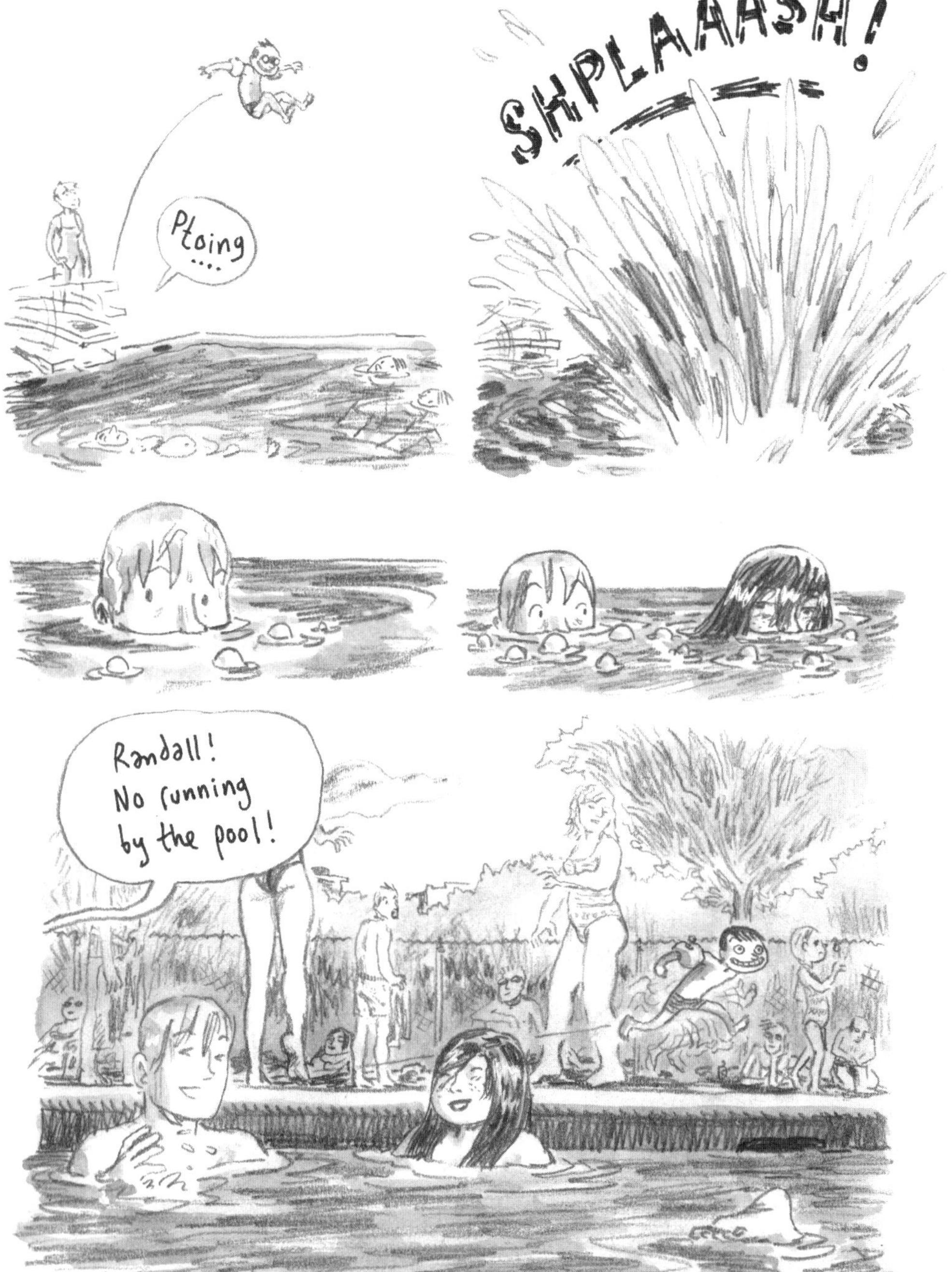
Ptoing ....
SHPLAAASH!
Randall! No running by the pool!

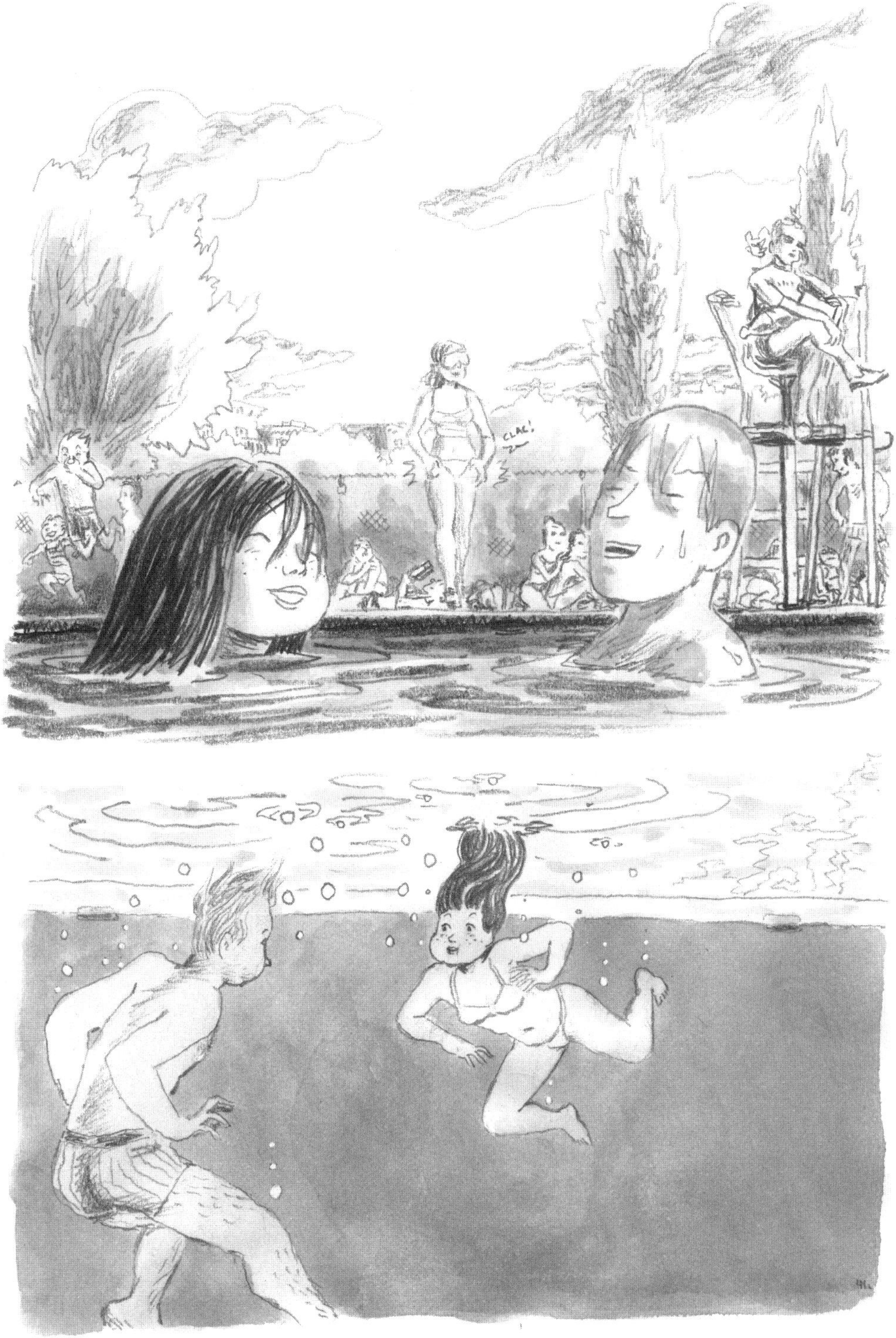
CLAC!

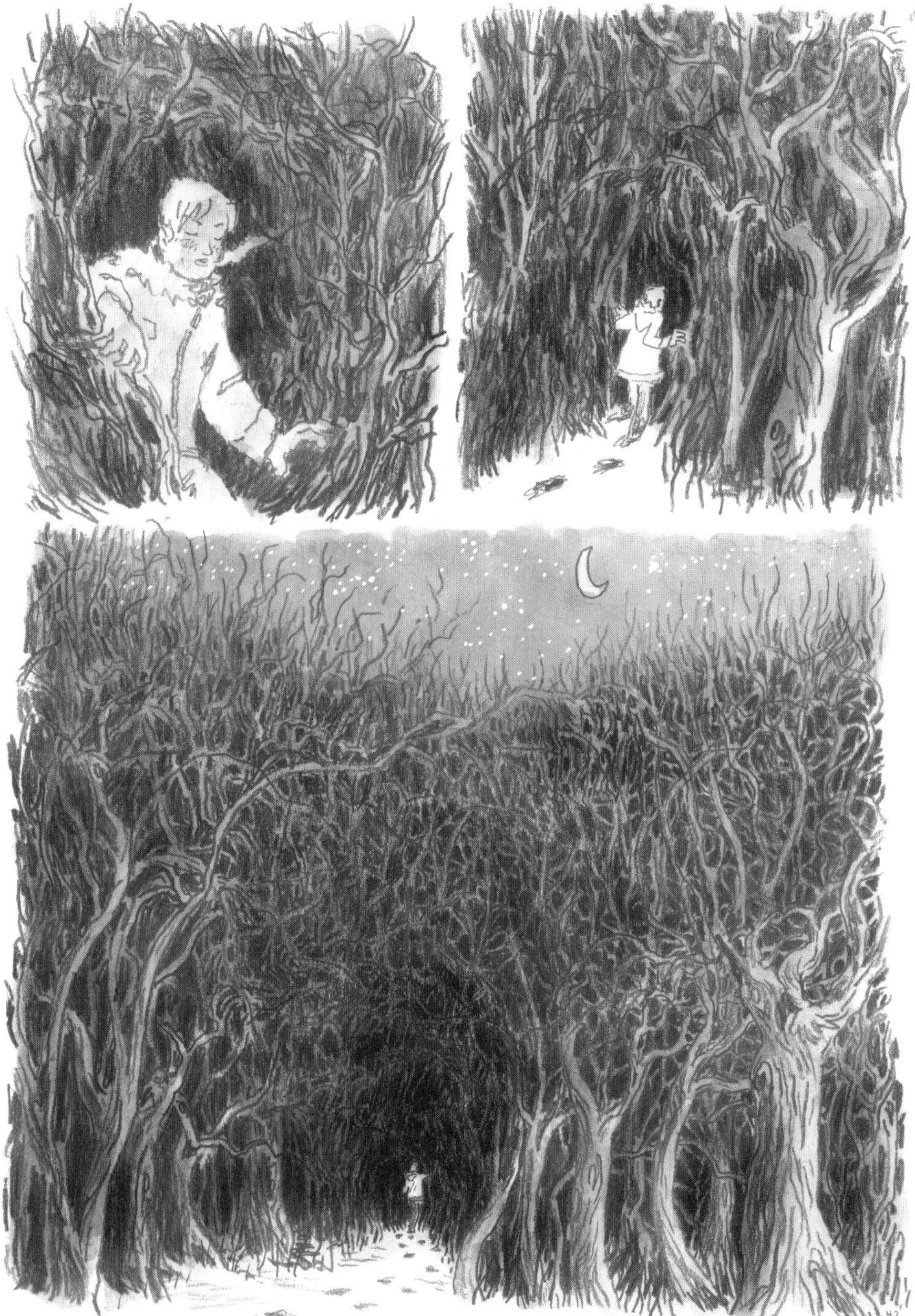

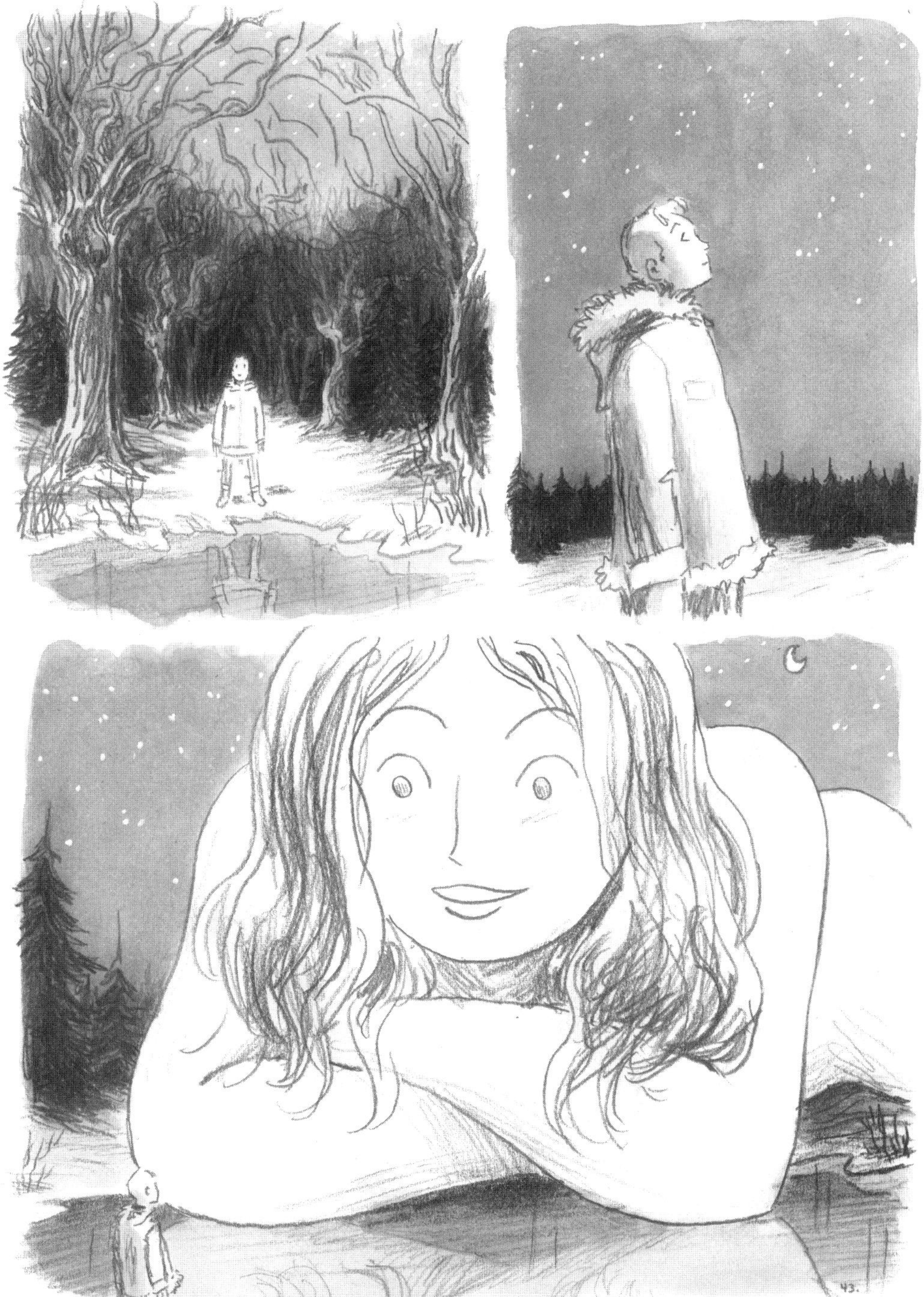

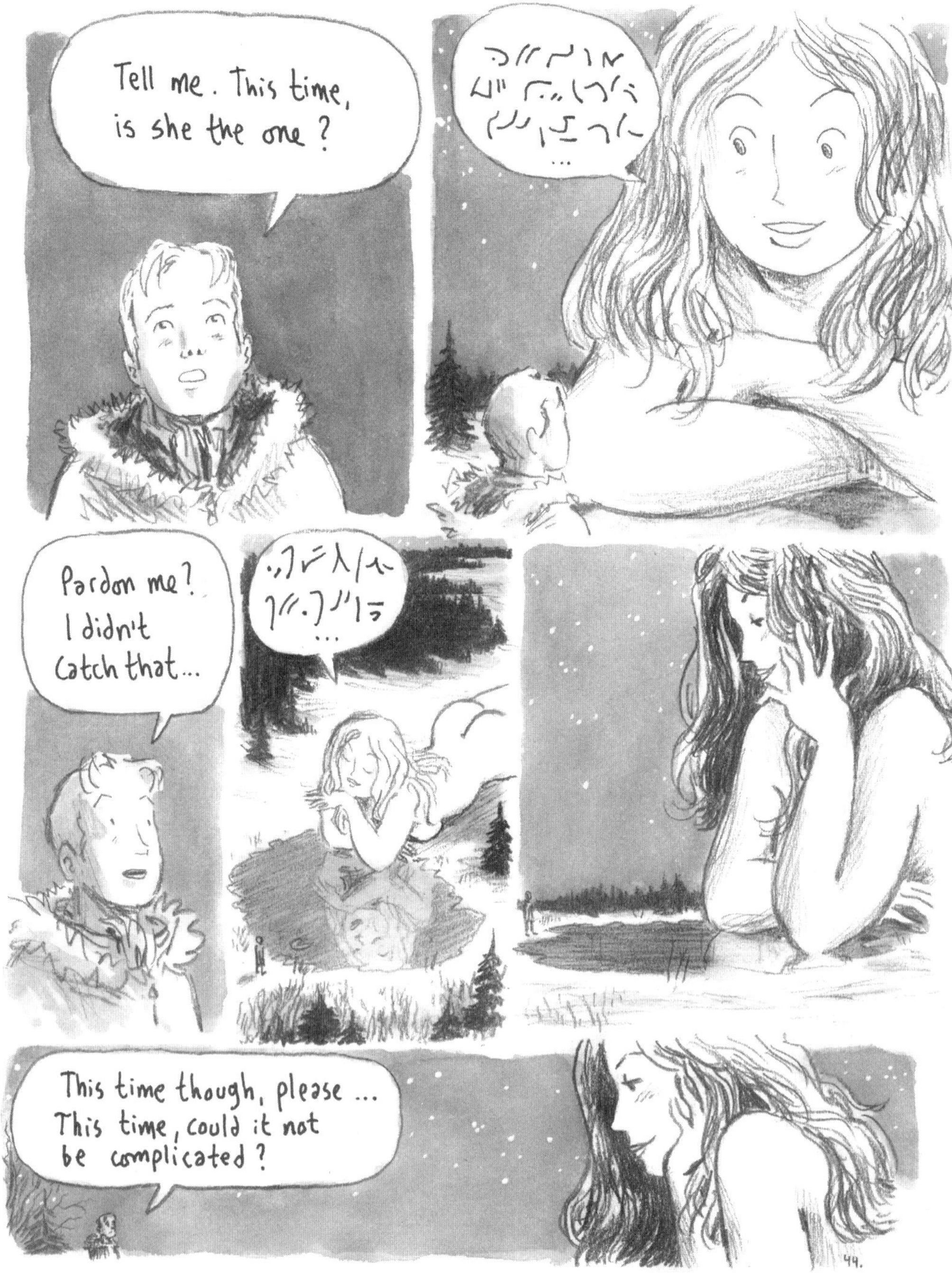
Tell me. This time, is she the one?
Pardon me? I didn't catch that...
This time though, please... This time, could it not be complicated?

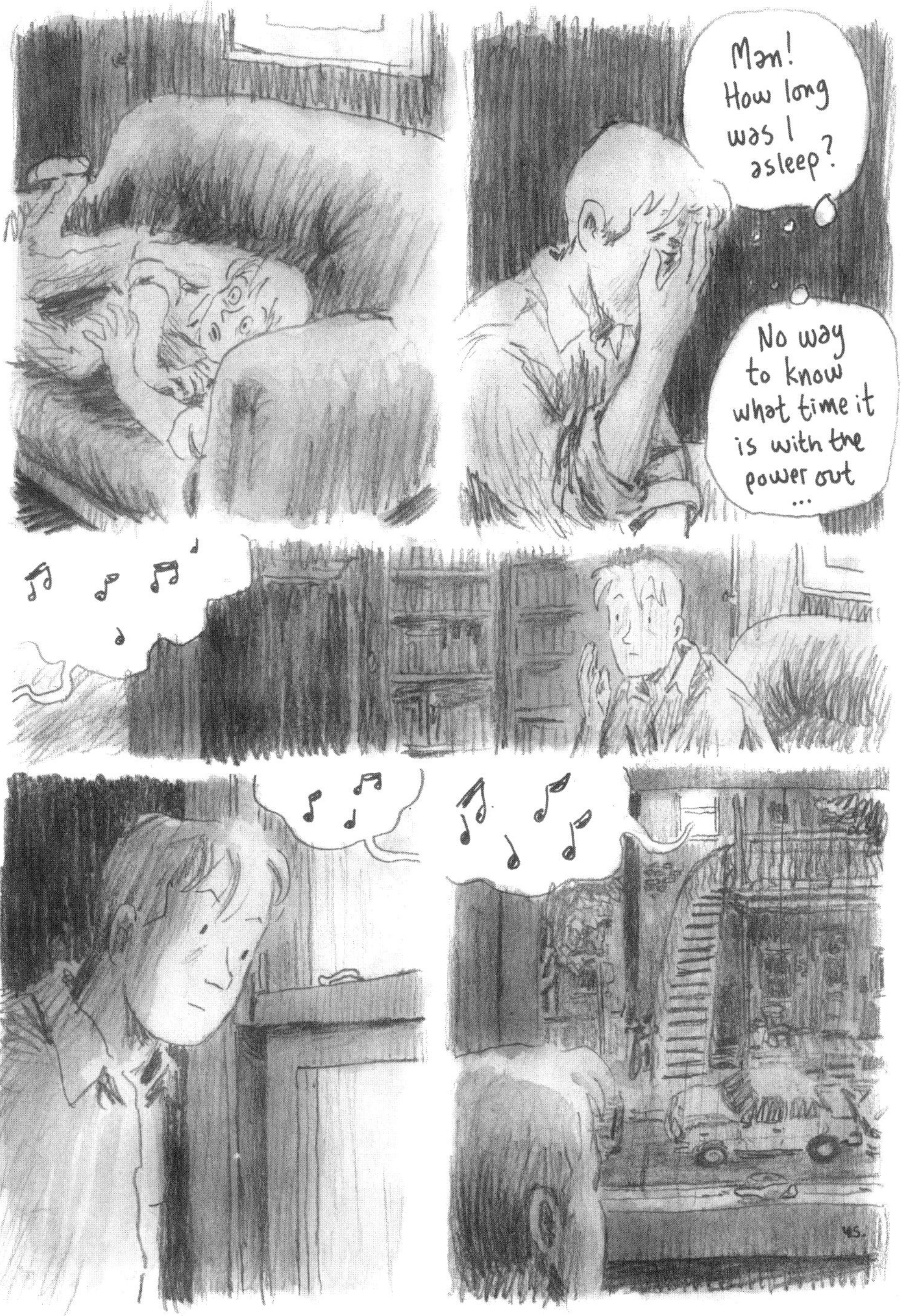
Man! How long was I asleep?
No way to know what time it is with the power out ...
M.S.

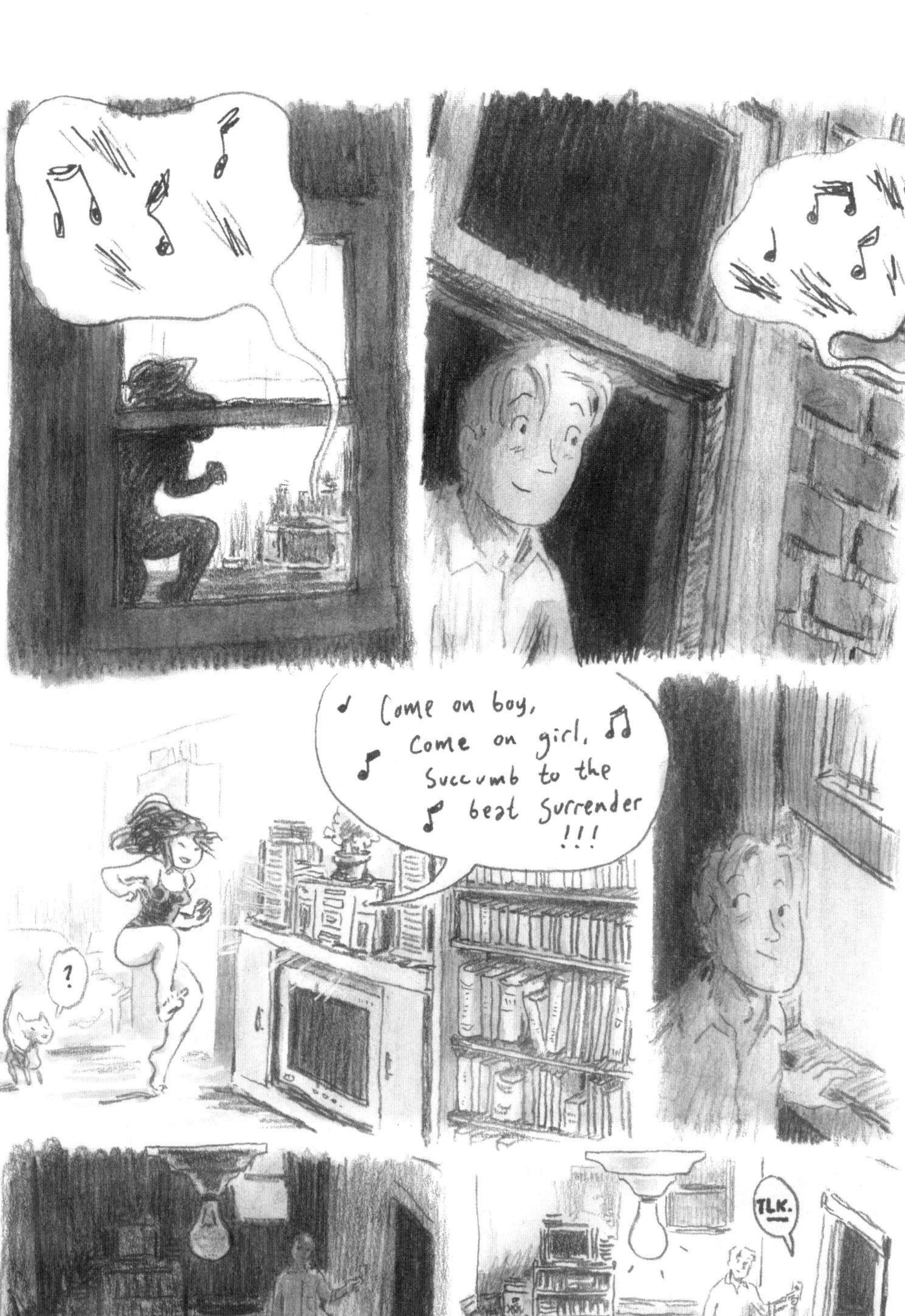
Come on boy,
Come on girl,
Succumb to the
beat Surrender
!!!
?
TLK.

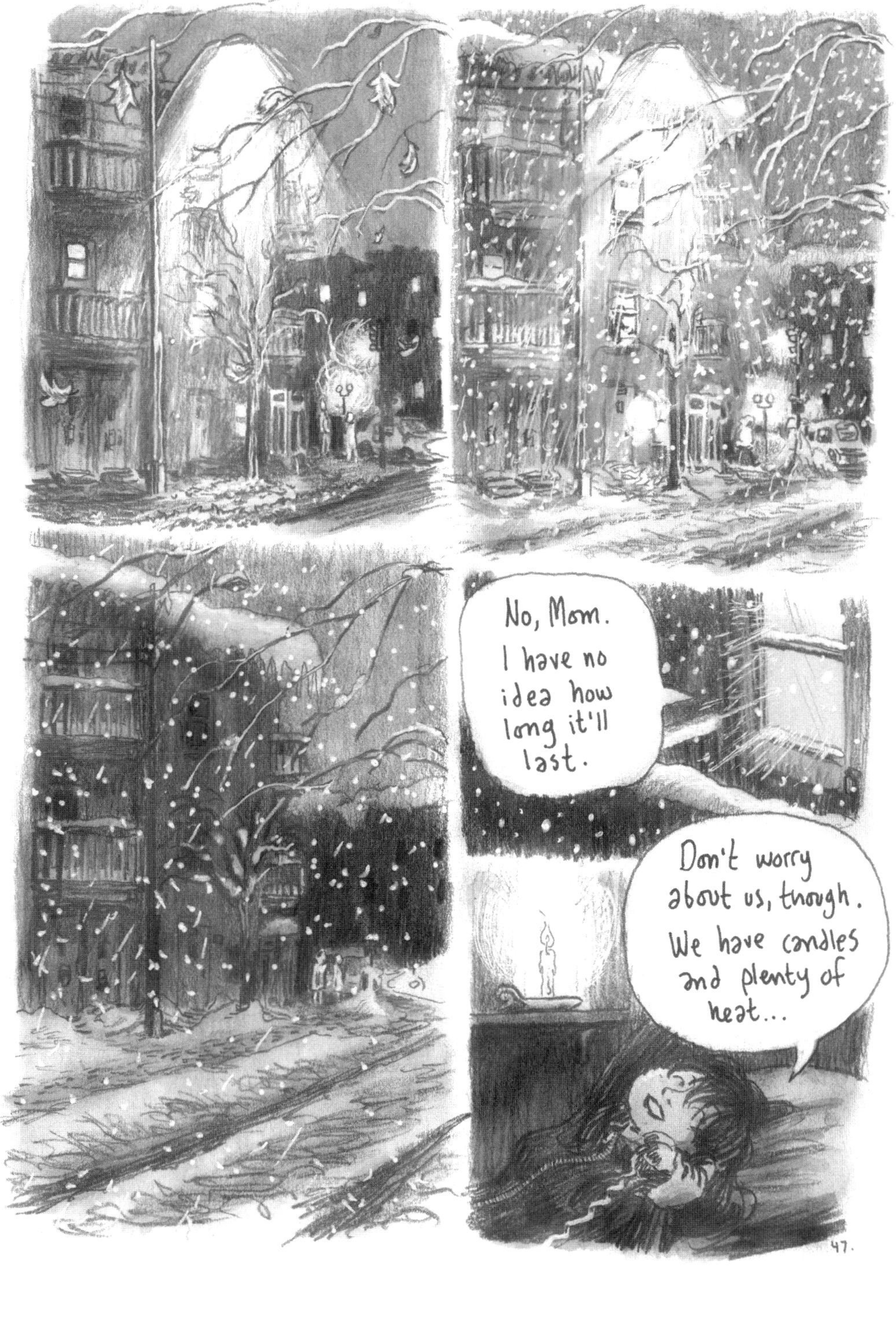
No, Mom. I have no idea how long it'll last.
Don't worry about us, though. We have candles and plenty of heat...

Oh! And guess what! I finally convinced Simon to change his haircut!
YESSSS!!!
Gna gna gna...
That's right. No more 80s gangster haircut! He looks very handsome!
Well, I've gotta go. And please, don't worry about us. Really!
Gnagn-rrrrr...

Yes, Mom... If the power stays out much longer, we'll go sleep at your place... OK. Bye, then... Bye...
It's funny. For most couples, it's a song or a place that makes them get all marshmallow-mushy and nostalgic about how they met... For us, it's power outages.

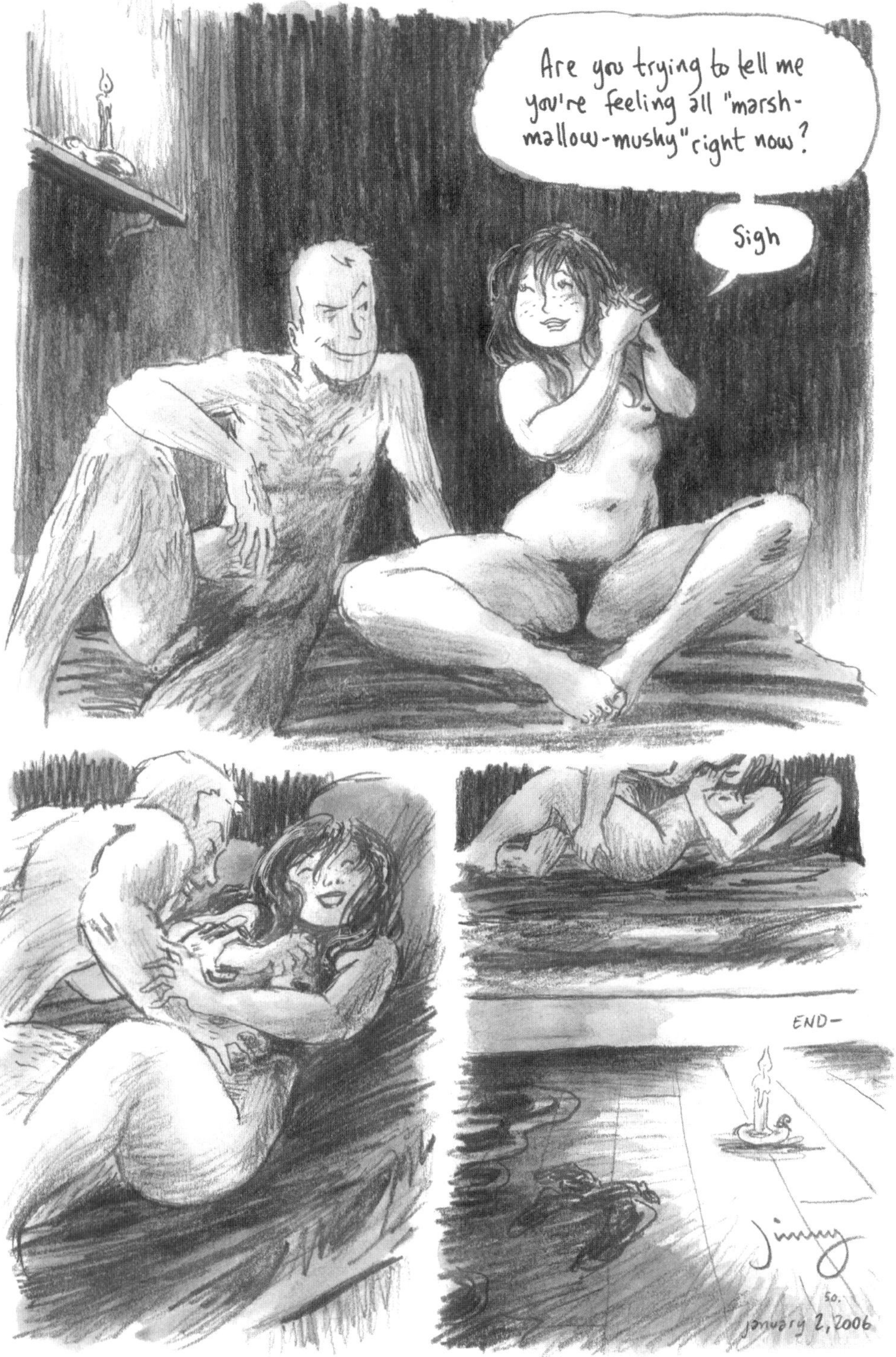
Are you trying to tell me you're feeling all "marsh-mallow-mushy" right now?
Sigh
END-
january 2, 2006

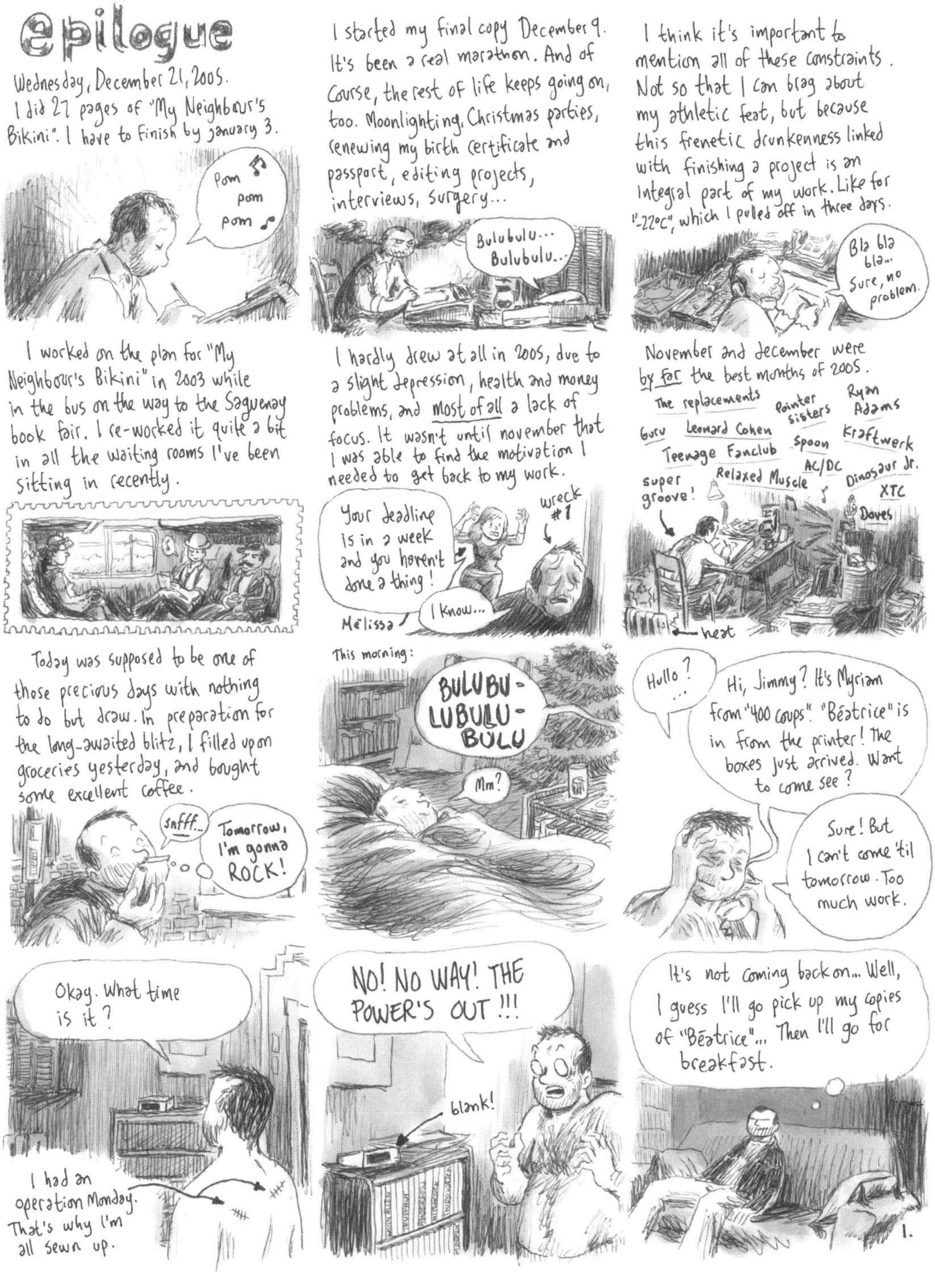
epilogue
Wednesday, December 21, 2005.
I did 27 pages of "My Neighbour's Bikini". I have to finish by january 3.
Pom pom pom
I started my final copy December 9. It's been a real marathon. And of course, the rest of life keeps going on, too. Moonlighting, Christmas parties, renewing my birth certificate and passport, editing projects, interviews, surgery...
Bulubulu... Bulubulu...
I think it's important to mention all of these constraints. Not so that I can brag about my athletic feat, but because this frenetic drunkenness linked with finishing a project is an integral part of my work. Like for "-22°C", which I pulled off in three days.
Bla bla bla... Sure, no problem.
I worked on the plan for "My Neighbour's Bikini" in 2003 while in the bus on the way to the Saguenay book fair. I re-worked it quite a bit in all the waiting rooms I've been sitting in recently.
I hardly drew at all in 2005, due to a slight depression, health and money problems, and most of all a lack of focus. It wasn't until november that I was able to find the motivation I needed to get back to my work.
Your deadline is in a week and you haven't done a thing!
wreck #1
I know...
Mélissa
November and december were by far the best months of 2005.
The replacements
Pointer sisters
Ryan Adams
Guru
Leonard Cohen
Spoon
Kraftwerk
Teenage Fanclub
AC/DC
Relaxed Muscle
Dinosaur Jr.
XTC
Doves
super groove!
heat
Today was supposed to be one of those precious days with nothing to do but draw. In preparation for the long-awaited blitz, I filled up on groceries yesterday, and bought some excellent coffee.
snfff...
Tomorrow, I'm gonna ROCK!
This morning:
BULUBU-LUBULU-BULU
Mm?
Hullo? ...
Hi, Jimmy? It's Myriam from "400 coups". "Béatrice" is in from the printer! The boxes just arrived. Want to come see?
Sure! But I can't come 'til tomorrow. Too much work.
Okay. What time is it?
I had an operation Monday. That's why I'm all sewn up.
NO! NO WAY! THE POWER'S OUT!!!
blank!
It's not coming back on... Well, I guess I'll go pick up my copies of "Béatrice"... Then I'll go for breakfast.

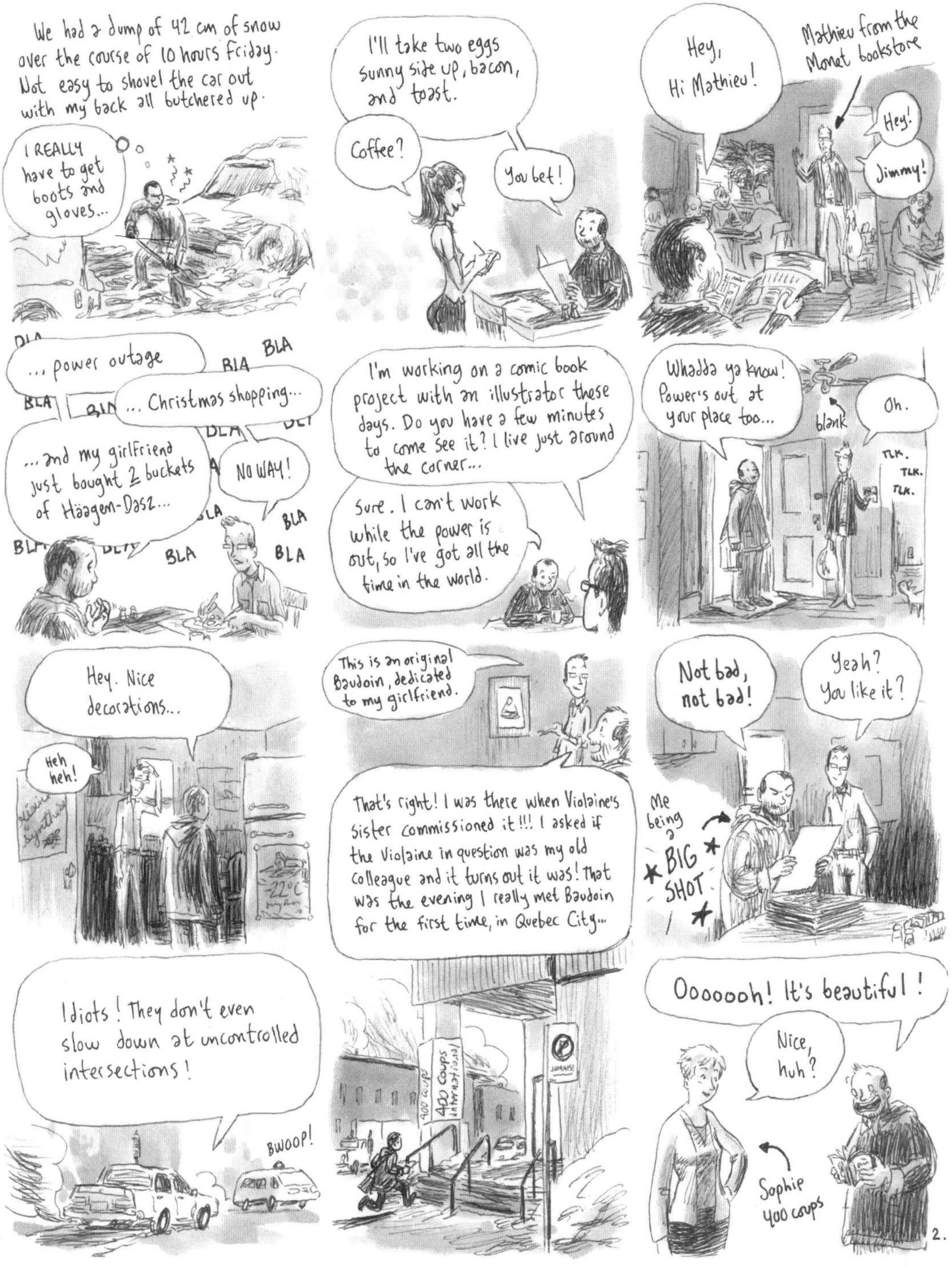

We had a dump of 42 cm of snow over the course of 10 hours Friday. Not easy to shovel the car out with my back all butchered up.
I REALLY have to get boots and gloves...
I'll take two eggs sunny side up, bacon, and toast.
Coffee?
You bet!
Hey, Hi Mathieu!
Mathieu from the Monet bookstore
Hey!
Jimmy!
... power outage
... Christmas shopping...
... and my girlfriend just bought 2 buckets of Häagen-Dasz...
NO WAY!
BLA
BLA
BLA
BLA
BLA
I'm working on a comic book project with an illustrator these days. Do you have a few minutes to come see it? I live just around the corner...
Sure. I can't work while the power is out, so I've got all the time in the world.
Whadda ya know! Power's out at your place too...
Oh.
blank
TLK.
TLK.
TLK.
Hey. Nice decorations...
Heh heh!
This is an original Baudoin, dedicated to my girlfriend.
That's right! I was there when Violaine's sister commissioned it!!! I asked if the Violaine in question was my old colleague and it turns out it was! That was the evening I really met Baudoin for the first time, in Quebec City...
Not bad, not bad!
Yeah? You like it?
Me being a BIG SHOT
Idiots! They don't even slow down at uncontrolled intersections!
BWOOP!
400 Coups
Ooooooh! It's beautiful!
Nice, huh?
Sophie 400 coups

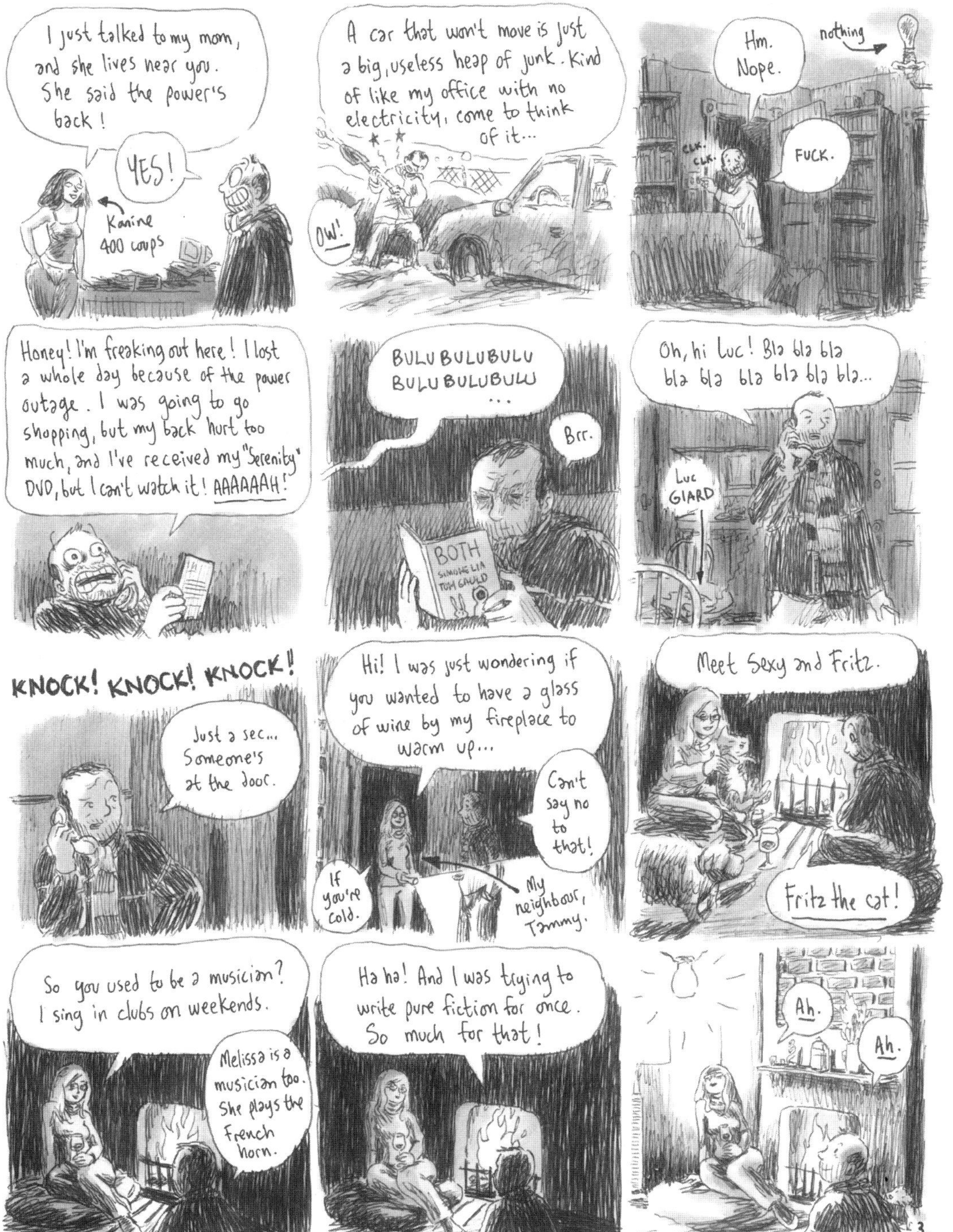

I just talked to my mom, and she lives near you. She said the power's back!
YES!
Karine
400 coups
A car that won't move is just a big, useless heap of junk. Kind of like my office with no electricity, come to think of it...
OW!
Hm. Nope.
nothing
CLK. CLK.
FUCK.
Honey! I'm freaking out here! I lost a whole day because of the power outage. I was going to go shopping, but my back hurt too much, and I've received my "Serenity" DVD, but I can't watch it! AAAAAAH!
BULUBULUBULU BULUBULUBULU ...
Brr.
BOTH
Oh, hi Luc! Bla bla bla bla bla bla bla bla bla...
Luc GIARD
KNOCK! KNOCK! KNOCK!
Just a sec... Someone's at the door.
Hi! I was just wondering if you wanted to have a glass of wine by my fireplace to warm up...
Can't say no to that!
If you're cold.
My neighbour, Tammy.
Meet Sexy and Fritz.
Fritz the cat!
So you used to be a musician? I sing in clubs on weekends.
Melissa is a musician too. She plays the French horn.
Ha ha! And I was trying to write pure fiction for once. So much for that!
Ah.
Ah.

January 4, '06 J.

René
1988 - 2006

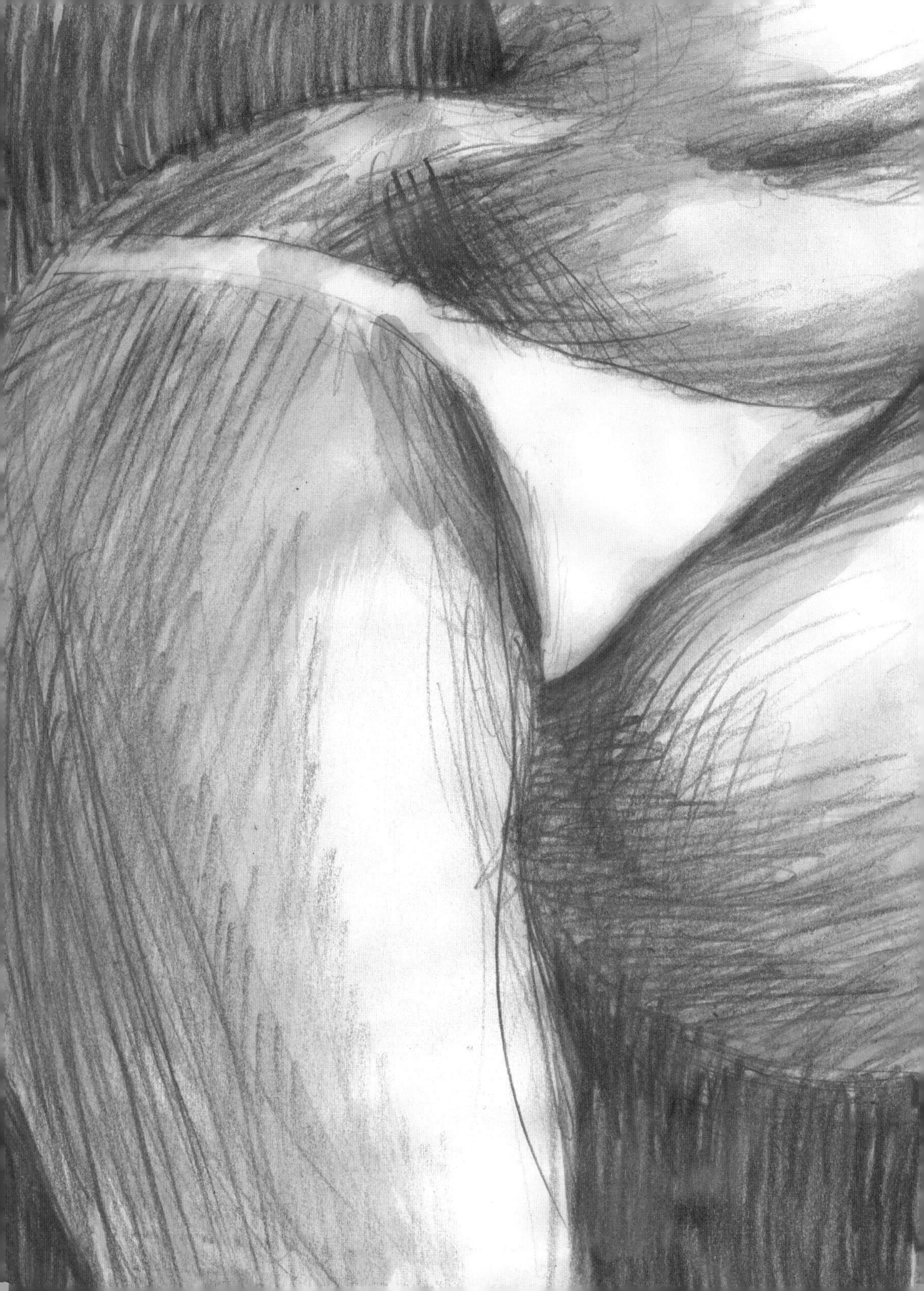